weddings
Valentine
style

weddings
Valentine
style

Diann Valentine

with Tonya Bolden

ATRIA BOOKS

New York   London   Toronto   Sydney

ATRIA BOOKS

1230 Avenue of the Americas

New York, NY 10020

Library of Congress Cataloging-in-Publication Data

Valentine, Diann.

   Weddings Valentine style / Diann Valentine with Tonya Bolden.

      p.   cm.

   1. Weddings—Planning. 2. Wedding etiquette. I. Title.

HQ745.V35 2006

395.2'2—dc22   2005048102

ISBN-13: 978-0-7434-9747-3
ISBN-10:   0-7434-9747-3

First Atria Books hardcover edition January 2006

10 9 8 7 6 5 4 3 2 1

ATRIA BOOKS is a trademark of Simon & Schuster, Inc.

Design by Julian Peploe

Manufactured in China

For information about special discounts for bulk purchases,
please contact Simon & Schuster Special Sales:
1-800-456-6798 or business@simonandschuster.com.

For Angel Baby

And let us not be weary in well doing:

for in due season we shall reap,

if we faint not.

—Galatians 6:9

contents

weddings
Valentine
style

beginnings:

when did I fall in love with
love?

The summer of 1977, in humid-heavy Shreveport, Louisiana, with my favorite cousin, Fuzzy—the brother I never had—I turned seven. Fuzzy and I had a ball, hanging out at the neighborhood swimming pool, feasting on penny candy from the corner store. This was my vacation, a break from my family's home in East Oakland Hills, California.

At summer's end, when I returned to California, home was no longer that three-story, four-bedroom wonder house (think *The Brady Bunch*) with two fireplaces, a large den, a wet bar and pool table in the basement, and in the backyard, an Olympic-size pool where I spent much of my free time practicing and perfecting my dive.

It was the only home I had known, having shared it with my parents and much older sisters, Julie and Mickie, who were by then out of the nest. That house was where Pop, a real estate entrepreneur and ace contractor, helped me with my homework weeknights, and on weekends, I helped him clean the pool and watched him weed, rake leaves, and be Mr. Fix-It. (He could fix *anything*.) That house was where, evening upon evening, I watched Mom make sumptuous dinners (mostly soul food sensations), while I pitched in— washing collards and pinto beans, stirring pots on the stove—as I listened to her recipes for being ladylike: "Ladies always sit with their legs crossed." "Ladies keep their elbows off the table." "Ladies take small bites, and anything on their forks should be able to fit inside their mouths without touching their lips because . . . when a lady finishes her meal, her lipstick should still be intact." I listened more out of respect than interest, never imagining that one day I would live by Mom's maxims.

And it was in that East Oakland Hills house that I had delighted in my parents' passion for entertaining—dinner parties, pool parties, barbecues, neighborhood talent shows. I worked my little magic on tea parties and sleepovers for friends and movie nights with my family.

After my summer with Fuzzy, home for my mother and me was a two-bedroom condo in downtown Oakland. My parents had separated; divorce was written in stone. My life would go split screen: weekdays with Mom, weekends with Pop. *Valentine?* My last name seemed a cruel joke.

So when did I fall in love with love? It was when, in rebellion against the perceived failure of my parents to fulfill my expectations, I declared, *When I have my own family, we'll stay together* forever.

My mother got remarried, to an enterprising, adventurous man, Joaquin Gabriel, when I was nine. My first response to this new addition to the family was to commit random acts of spite. He persevered in his attempt to love me, despite my behavior, and I ultimately grew to count him among my blessings.

Joaquin, being Filipino, brought new foods and flavors into my life. My young soul food–oriented palate became accustomed to monkfish and *lots* of other fish I'd never tasted, along with chicken adobo, *lumpia* (Filipino egg rolls), *pan de leche,* and shredded coconut rice cakes. I quickly adapted, though rice with *every* meal I did not get.

Thanks to Mom and Joaquin's love of travel, I also savored a variety of other cultures and scenes—the U.S. Virgin Islands, Mexico, Puerto Rico, St. Bart's, Korea. By the time I was thirteen years old, I was coming out of my shyness and into some leadership skills—serving as class president in seventh, eighth, and ninth grades; organizing fund-raisers, dances, and other school events. My guiding light was Principal Carolyn Getridge—so stylish and with such a Gucci-bag jones. More important, Principal Getridge possessed a diamond mind, and she was so eager to mentor me, her protégée, whom she gifted one fall with a Gucci bag—my first. She had picked it up while vacationing in Italy. And, yes, it still remains in my possession.

By sweet sixteen, school was the last thing on my mind. *Lovestruck!* He was five years my senior—a *real* man, I thought—the man of my dreams. He gave me a cell phone; he had a fly ride. The reality? We were more like oil and vinegar, and our mix did not make for a well-balanced vinaigrette. But I was so hungry for love, I tried over and over to make the doomed-for-failure recipe work.

At the same time, a part of my soul was also striving to make something of myself. I entered college, majoring in marketing, minoring in African-American studies, and yearned for something more on my horizon than just "a good job," as Pop had counseled.

I discovered a way to achieve more than a job when my cousin Shelly asked eighteen-year-old me to help her plan her wedding. *This could be a business*, I thought. My next move was to enroll in a wedding consultant certification program. The following year, I launched Memories.

Weddings are a billion-dollar industry. Wedding magazines are thick with advertisements for businesses providing any and every thing a bride could want. I studied the market and was annoyed by the wedding industry's blatant

disregard of black brides. *How dare they dismiss us! How dare they ignore our money!* In bridal magazine after bridal magazine, hardly ever did I see even a lousy black cake-top couple or a menu with some soul going on. *I'll be for the invisible ones.*

My early clients were pink- and blue-collar workers (bank tellers, postal workers, bus drivers) looking for fresh flourishes in the design of their dream day. Relatively modest budgets notwithstanding, I did my best to deliver élan (I was swagging rooms when such was a rarity for workaday folk). I brainstormed like crazy on ways to make even small elements of a client's I-Do day unique.

No matter how small a client's budget, I pulled out all the stops and let my creative energies flow to find a florist, caterer, and wedding-cake baker who could fulfill my client's vision. And I was by her side from shop to bridal shop, every step of the way. I was in my bliss when doing whatever it took to tailor a wedding to a woman's best style and her soul's singular song.

As I look back, I marvel at how I was able to give my clients the best while still wrapped up in the madness that was my own personal life. Then again, Memories was my refuge as I stayed in a stormy relationship, then ended up pregnant.

I'm gonna make it work—this love's gonna live! I made myself believe it. I wanted my own family *so* bad.

I was in my bliss when doing whatever it took to tailor a wedding to a woman's best style and her soul's singular song.

Then came *pre*-partum depression. Then ten, twenty, sixty-five pounds piled on. I went down—on my knees, praying for guidance and strength. My parents had never been churchgoers, but my paternal grandmother was. It was she who had often taken me to her Baptist church. In doing so, Grandma Mary seeded in me a longing for the holy. She taught me how to pray.

When my daughter was born, I prayed. *She's going to have her daddy!* And I *stayed.* Left him. Went back. Stayed. Prayed. Then, in the summer of 1991, he was the one who "moved on." I juggled full-time college and a full-time job as a bookkeeper at a grocery store, and kept sight of a bright future for my daughter and me.

God, if I can't have my own family, how can I just be a part of love? Just let me see it, be around it, I prayed.

My clientele expanded—a doctor's daughter, a lawyer's daughter, a few Oakland athletes—more through word-of-mouth than advertising. I organized African American Brides of Distinction in 1994, the first such bridal trade show in California. The event was more successful than I had imagined it would be. I did a repeat in 1995. Both times, sisters turned out in huge numbers. Vendors, too. *Yes!* But both expos left me in the red. By 1996 I was praying for a way out, an escape from the city of so many disappointments and hard lessons.

A party I produced at San Francisco's Planet Hollywood for Golden State Warrior Joe Smith's foundation prompted Smith's agent to offer me a job as event planner for his sports marketing firm in L.A. I packed up quick, and in August 1996, with my 1988 Honda Accord EX, a mattress, two suitcases of clothes, and my thirty-six-inch floor-model television, I was on my way to L.A. Pop rode shotgun and played moving man. Mom had agreed to take care of my daughter until I got settled.

Every Friday evening I hopped Southwest Airlines' seven-o'clock to Oakland to see my baby; every Monday morning, the six-o'clock back to L.A. A hundred bucks round-trip, weekend after weekend. The job turned out not to be a dream. I quit after a few months, ready to return to Oakland.

"I hate it here!" I sobbed over the phone to my father one autumn evening. "I'm coming home for good. I miss my baby!"

"Just relax," Pop said. "Calm down. Give yourself time to figure out what you really want to do." Like a true real estate owner, he reminded me that I had signed a six-month lease and did not need the drama of lease breaking.

"When your lease is up in January, if you still want to come home, fine. I'll even come get you." How typical of Pop: ever there for me with sound advice *and* a helping hand. I followed his advice. I calmed down. I started temping as well. I found a church home and grew spiritually. I asked God, "Where am I to be?" "What am I to do?" As Christmas neared, I read God's silence as a sign to leave L.A. But on December 23, a friend called with a lead on a job: assistant in the marketing department of a major entertainment company. Christmas Eve I had the interview; later that day, the job.

Stay was the message. With a solid job, it wasn't long before I was able to bring my baby girl to L.A.

Word of my event planning in the Bay Area reached people in L.A. The party I had produced for Joe Smith's foundation had received rave reviews. But the gateway into the world of entertainers was a jazz-themed wedding I produced for an R&B singer. The venue was a 140-foot yacht, which sailed from Jack London Square in Oakland to San Francisco and then down the coast and back.

By the time my first L.A. celebrity came calling, I had shed Memories and renamed my enterprise D. R. Valentine & Associates with the high hope of making the most of my name. I wanted to start building a brand and get people used to seeing Valentine associated with weddings.

My first L.A. celeb celebration was to be held on a spring afternoon at a private estate just outside the city. Circumstances beyond my clients' control prompted them to relocate and scale back the event. Poof went my dream of designing a truly opulent wedding. Then, in April 1998, actress Lela Rochon called. She was interviewing candidates to produce a grand celebration of her wedding—Yes!—to film director Antoine Fuqua.

Left: Me and Mom—the person most responsible for my grace notes.

Right: Me and Pop—my anchor, bringing me back down to earth whenever I become untethered.

Passionate

My daughter, Riann—my Angel Baby.
She is my greatest accomplishment
and most prized creation.

Never let them
see you sweat.

Though the meeting went great, afterward I thought, There's no way Lela is going to hire *me*. When I didn't hear back from her after a few months, I figured for sure she had opted for an over-the-top, big-shot Hollywood wedding planner. Wasn't I stunned when, about six months later, I got a callback. Lela and I hit the ground running. The wedding was six months away—and she hadn't yet wrapped up her work in the film *Any Given Sunday*.

Lela and Antoine—what impeccable taste! Between her flair for glamour and his keen eye for architecture and lighting—what a fantasia of possibilities! Especially after I convinced Lela that L.A.'s Immanuel Presbyterian Church was not too grand for her. Its main sanctuary's many glories include eighty-foot-tall vaulted ceilings.

The possibilities we made realities included yards and yards of white velvet, adorned by tulips, scalloping the ninety-seven-foot-long center aisle. Fifteen hundred calla lilies in six huge arrangements graced the altar. White candles on six-foot-tall candelabras towered at every other pew. As Lela and Antoine's three-hundred-plus guests entered the church, each received a petite sterling silver (cool) or brass (warm) bell, to be tinkled as the couple made their exuberant way down the aisle as husband and wife to an original score by Emmy Award–winning composer Earl Rose.

When guests arrived at L.A.'s Biltmore Hotel, a Beaux-Arts treasure, they were no doubt expecting the typical reception with beautiful linens and centerpieces. But Lela and Antoine had given me carte blanche to give the Biltmore's Crystal Ballroom an extreme makeover— Old Hollywood style. The makeover included recarpeting the entire ballroom white, covering the dated-looking curtains on the balconies, and installing a custom white patent leather dance floor. The mirrors atop guest tables were not for checking your lipstick. Whenever people looked down at the table, they were looking up at the frescoes Giovanni Smeraldi created for the hotel's opening in 1923.

As the doors of the Crystal Ballroom opened and guests streamed in, I was tucked in a corner on pins and needles. I felt I had done great work, but I knew that the true seal of approval would come from the guests—Vivica A. Fox, Rob Schneider, Angela Bassett, Terry McMillan, and Star Jones among them.

There were oohs and aahs and many an "Oh my God!" This from people no strangers to ritzy events. *Yes!*

All these years later, I still well up when I remember those reactions to my work, when I remember, too, that at that moment I knew my prayers asking to be around people in love had been answered, knew that my enterprise was more than a refuge. I had come into my destiny, my calling: producing weddings, Valentine style.

At that moment I knew . . . I had come into
my destiny, my calling: producing weddings,
Valentine style.

Hollywood glamour at its finest.

color
correct

The first thing on the average woman's mind, after she says *Yes!* to the big question, is finding that perfect wedding dress.

And so, she's off—dog-earing and sticky-pad flagging page after page of a gazillion bridal magazines. Mostly, what she beholds is a bounty of exquisite wedding dresses on women who look more like a Nicole Kidman than an Erykah Badu. And the models are generally barely a size two.

Often, the lady in love also finds herself so blinded by white that she fails to do a color check—forgets that she is probably like most black women: a style maven, a fashionista, someone who is able to wear color well. What a pity to waste an asset.

Remember *Coming to America*? It's my favorite wedding movie—love the costumes! When Imani Izzi (Vanessa Bell Calloway), the betrothed of Prince Akeem (Eddie Murphy), arrives at the palace—what a splendor: her rich, dark chocolate skin—oh, how aglow in a long-sleeved, ankle-length, form-fitting, twenty-foot-train gown of gold leaf and jewel-encrusted appliqués. I still covet those eight-inch gold coil bracelets.

Everyone in DeLeon and Gary's party had
a chance to lounge in six inches of rose
petals—but only after the ceremony.

World wedding-dress history has color! color! everywhere—gem-toned damask silks; pastel satins embroidered
with flowers and butterflies; ruby red and night black velvets,
sometimes bedecked with diamonds, sapphires, and other
precious gems, sometimes trimmed in ermine or sable. Do
you think a white wedding dress is the aboriginal tradition in
Kuala Lumpur or Timbuktu? Some Japanese marry in red;
East Indians, in pink saris bordered in gold and silver.

Some credit Anne of Brittany as the trailblazer in the
white-for-wedding construct when, in 1499, she married
France's Louis XII in all white. Then, in 1840 Queen Victoria
wore all white when she wed her cousin Prince Albert, and
the whole "married in white, you have chosen right,"
became vogue. Is Queen Victoria in your family tree?

If you are a virgin and you hold to the notion of white
as a symbol of purity and you want to proclaim yours, it's

Chanté Moore chose just the right shade of
taupe for her skin tone.

Ever dreamed of a wedding dress
constructed of all flowers?

Above: Here's a woman who knows how to
dress for a celebration.

Opposite: Even I could not deny how wonderful
Sharhonda looked in white.

your day. (If you are not a virgin, why the pretense?) I am not totally opposed to white-for-wedding; I just know that many black women do not look their best in stark white.

Why not pretty in pink? Many shades of black click with that color—and not just the light-skinned like Shari Headley, who played Lisa, Prince Akeem's true love from America: enchanting as she floats toward her man in a voluminous cloud of sheerest pink drenched with iridescent

flecks. How sweet the strapless fitted bodice and full skirt. How breathtaking the shirred thirty-foot train.

Why not a red that sets off your flaming locks? Champagne makes hazel eyes pop. Mint green flatters the fair-skinned and green-eyed. Caramel skin looks dreamy in canary yellow and shades of gold. Consider how stunning a chocolate brown woman with a full head of gray will look in pure platinum. (On the other hand, certain blues and purples deprive many a sister of her glow.) What color, what shade enhances your beauty?

In your search for style, do not make bridal magazines and bridal shops your first and last stops. "I want you to put aside every bridal magazine you have purchased," I typically tell a client at the outset. "Blot images of your best friend's wedding from your mind." I say, move to your own beat. Check out your favorite designer's line of ball gowns (many also have wedding gowns). Richard Tyler? Badgley Mischka? Valentino? Versace? Dolce & Gabanna? Zac Posen? Tom Ford?

What silhouette best suits you? The traditional gown with the full skirt can be a fantastic fit if you are on the slimmer side. If you are not small-boned and slender, a full skirt may make you appear larger than you care to look. If that's you and you must have a full skirt, make it a dropped waist: it will elongate your torso and accentuate your curves.

"Blot images of your best friend's wedding from your mind." I say, move to your own beat.

You are the centerpiece of your celebration.

Opposite: Sara's nephew stole the heart of
every woman who attended her wedding.

Sheaths are a formal alternative to the traditional wedding gown. The body-hugging form looks amazing on women who have curves and are not afraid to show them. Or go mermaid if you desire the sleekness of a sheath and the added drama of a flared bottom and train. A-line looks good on just about anyone and is a comfort zone for those who feel that they have a bit too much tummy. Got legs like Tina Turner? You may want to skip the gowns altogether. Head for the minis.

As you picture yourself in an ivory Nefertiti-inspired satin silhouette with a richly embroidered mitred hat, collar, and sash; a gauzy night-in-Tunisia-styled caftan; a sapphire blue silk semi-sari delight; or even a snazzy slate two-piece tailored evening suit with jeweled buttons, keep location in mind. Is your heart set on saying "I do" on a beach at dawn? High noon in a two-hundred-year-old cathedral? A garden at teatime? Overlooking a glittering city skyline at night? Will your reception be on grass or poolside, in a ballroom, on a yacht? Will you do the unusual and marry on a Friday evening or a Sunday afternoon?

Accessories

Your engagement ring may be all the jewelry you need. And a pair of studs, perhaps. When in doubt, keep it simple, especially if your dress is big and busy. Other than at the time of the garter-belt toss, hardly anyone gets a long look at your shoes. So if you marry in a gown, I say, don't sweat the shoes. (But this doesn't mean you have to default to dyeable peau-de-soie pumps.) What matters most is that the shoes complement your dress. Ideally, they should also be comfortable—but, oh, the sacrifices we will make in search of fashion satisfaction.

Are you a shoe queen? By all means, indulge.
Do what Patti LaBelle and *Sex and the City*'s Carrie
Bradshaw would do: head straight for some Manolo
Blahnik—or reach for some Jimmy Choo as April did
in search of the perfect pair of kicks to complement
her gold dress.

Express yourself!

aura

chapter 2

Getting to know her. That's my first duty to a client: to look, listen, observe, and absorb as much as I can about her. More than the "facts." I'm poised to see the beautiful mind behind the pretty face, the soul of a poet at the core of the no-nonsense entrepreneur. I try to be as attentive to her silences as I am to her words, from the moment we start talking through her ideal look for her special day. After a client has made the major decisions about her wedding attire, we turn our attention to ceremony and reception location.

Every space has a spirit, a voice. When venue shopping, keep in mind Goethe's declaration that "architecture is frozen music." So, as I look at a church or private estate, I also listen. I take in the walls, doorways, moldings, light fixtures—I never fight the architecture, whether art nouveau or rococo. I never work against the aura of a space. I listen for the song.

Does a room whisper for cool colors? Or does it shout out, "Yes, I'm eggshell now, but dream me in saffron and watch me bust a move!" Does a balcony beg for bunting or a waterfall of wisteria? Is an alcove in need of an arabesque of brassavola orchids? A plain, boxy room? I see it as a huge opportunity to *create*!

Pages 46 and 47: We used hues of baby blue and chocolate brown because Shawn and Sharhonda wanted an icy-cool feel to their celebration. As usual, Peter Otero worked his genius when it came to the centerpieces. White forsythia on ice? No—Peter wrapped large branches with dendrobium orchids, then stood the arrangements in trays of rough-cut opaque glass.

Below and opposite: The church's original carpeting was teal blue. Nice, but not quite right for Shawnee's color scheme, so we recarpeted the entire sanctuary with a residential carpet. As the wedding was on a July afternoon, the sunlight would have been almost blinding, thus the custom pink velvet drapes for the two-story cathedral windows. Because the church was so massive, anything we designed had to be as grand as its aura.

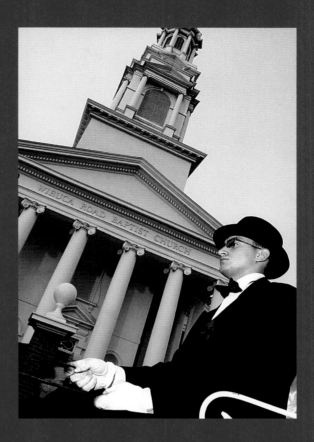

Opposite: Placing Shawnee and Jimmy's monogram on the drapes and adorning them with rose garland tiebacks was just one added touch.

Above: Shawnee and Jimmy's driver awaits them.

As I look and listen, my mind's eye is a kaleidoscope of design ideas. Later, I rummage through my treasury of clippings—floral designs, fabrics, trimmings, light fixtures, table treatments, interior spaces, china settings. I also turn to my first-choice sources for new inspirations: magazines such as *Vogue, InStyle, W, Elle Décor, Interior Design, Architectural Digest, Lighting Dimensions, Frame, Dwell,* and *Veranda.* Art books, too.

Often, I draw on something I have seen in my travels. Some weddings trigger flashbacks to my first time in Paris, to the sensation I had being in an atmosphere of romance. The spark was not provided by the people per se. It was rather in the finials, the stark elegance of the floors of the Louvre, the crown molding in the lobby of the Four Seasons hotel. Everywhere I looked, Paris absolutely exuded L-O-V-E—*love.*

As in Paris, so in other cities I have studied: astonishments crafted by stonecutters, wood- and wrought-iron workers, glaziers, and other artisans. Florence, with all the magic that Medici money made possible, is my favorite city (so far). There, and elsewhere in Italy, I visited cathedral after cathedral, soaking up the majesty of centuries-old ribbed ceilings, stained-glass windows, frescoes, and other marvels. In Moscow, it was St. Basil's Cathedral (surprise, surprise) with its festival of spired multicolored, bulbous, swirling cupolas and a scalloped central tower that most romanced my soul.

Whether in America or abroad, whenever I see a work of art, be it man-made (a Tudor cottage, an English garden) or God's creation (crystal-clear Caribbean blue water), I wonder, How can I incorporate some of this into my work? How can I offer a client at least an echo of this soaring greatness?

As we discuss and I meditate on a client's venue, I envision her dazzling in her bridal attire. Then I let my ideas and my client's desires marinate. When the vision becomes clear, crisp, I get busy, trusting that final touches and flourishes will reveal themselves with every move I make.

Some weddings trigger flashbacks to my first time in Paris, to the sensation I had being in an atmosphere of romance.

Rubus sanctus is the botanist's name for the bush
some identify as the burning bush of Exodus 3:
a bush that can live for a millennium, and which bears
flowers similar to roses and raspberry-like fruit.

And when the LORD saw that he turned aside to see, God called unto him out of the midst of the bush. . . . "Put off thy shoes from off thy feet; for the place whereon thou standest is holy ground."

A church was a must for DeLeon Richards when she and then L.A. Dodgers outfielder Gary Sheffield renewed their vows. *Holy! Holy! Holy!* That's what DeLeon wanted to resonate throughout her day. But no chubby cherub and dulcet lyre tones for her. This gospel great called for an ambience of Awesome-Almighty.

DeLeon chose to have the ceremony at First Presbyterian Church, in St. Petersburg, Florida, a simple white stucco structure with a broad front-gabled roof and Tudor doorway. But above that archway floats a striking relief sculpture of the burning bush.

. . . and he led the flock to the backside of the desert, and came to the mountain of God, even to Horeb.

The sanctuary was airy, its walls stark white. "Ornate" had not been the watchword. The sanctuary's simplicity conveyed a sense of sacred power, but for DeLeon's renewal I found it a little too subdued. DeLeon agreed; she was open to color. *Paint the walls burnt orange?* I wondered. *Adorn them with tapestries?* In the meantime, I focused on my initial inspiration: the burning bush.

And the angel of the LORD appeared unto him in a flame of fire out of the midst of a bush: and he looked, and, behold, the bush burned with fire, and the bush was not consumed.

I considered DeLeon's date and time: early February, at dusk, a time of ingathering, reflection. The revelation? Ten-foot-tall torchères swaddled in golden rose-petaled satin blankets would flank the church's doorway.

And Moses said, I will now turn aside, and see this great sight, why the bush is not burnt.

When the torchères were afire, the church façade would be awash with flickering flames; the bush would come alive.

And when the LORD saw that he turned aside to see, God called unto him out of the midst of the bush. . . . "Put off thy shoes from off thy feet; for the place whereon thou standest is holy ground."

I have to confess that I first thought the baptismal font in the center aisle was an eyesore. Then Walter Hubert, art director extraordinaire, pleaded for the font and himself: "Work with me!" Walter envisioned a red-rose-petal coverlet for the font, transforming it into a powerful punctuation point in the processionals. The female attendants would enter from the rear, the fellas from the side through a split in the pews, meeting up with their partners just beyond the font. The couples would continue to the front of the church and take their places at the altar. They would sit in chairs to keep pristine the

The altar was blanketed with the petals from seventy thousand roses. The five hundred custom candles, which ranged from one foot to five feet tall, haloed DeLeon and Gary during the ceremony.

rose petals that blanketed the floor. Only DeLeon and Gary would stand on the rose petals.

When DeLeon and her father walked up the aisle, they would stop at the baptismal-font-turned-rose-petal-mount. There, DeLeon would be in a ray of amber light from above, a light that would follow her as she continued with her father to Gary's side.

In the balcony above the sanctuary's entrance, we would install a fog machine to emit delicate clouds of smoke as guests took their seats.

. . . for the place whereon thou standest is holy ground.

Towering above the main entrance to the sanctuary, light streams in between the branches of the massive burning bush sculpture. BEHOLD!

My first dream-weaving session with Toni Braxton for the celebration of her marriage to musician Kierston "Keri" Lewis took place in her home in Atlanta, Georgia. Immediately, I could see that Toni Braxton possessed an appreciation of fine art, jewelry, china—fine *everything*. And she told me that the sweetest part of her run in the part of Belle in *Beauty and the Beast* on Broadway was having to wear glorious gowns. Toni wanted just such a gown in order to look and feel like a princess on her wedding day. She chose a Vera Wang ivory duchesse satin gown with a cathedral train and notched, crystal-beaded spaghetti-strap bodice.

When it came to location, Toni had her eye on Dean Gardens, a sixty-acre extravaganza just outside Atlanta. She wanted early spring. That April day was perfect for her ceremony. Andrew Young officiated in Dean Gardens' French rose garden. Following the ceremony, there was a cocktail hour near the fountains, then a reception near the estate's clamshell amphitheater.

An outdoor reception called for a tent. What kind? Circus-top tent? Frame? Custom? Toni's choice to be a "princess" in the great outdoors made such sense because in her I saw such a splendid blend of glamour and just-folks. (When the darling of high fashion named her firstborn Denim, I was not surprised.)

When we talked colors, Toni was dreaming tender shades of pink and blue. When she gave me a tour of her home so that I could learn more about her, I made note of gorgeous pink and red rose pavés gentling various rooms. I also noticed more than a few Tiffany boxes: gifts she had received, gifts she was preparing to send.

"You really have a thing for Tiffany."

The floodgates opened wide. "I *love* Tiffany," said Toni. She had Tiffany bone china and porcelain tableware, Tiffany crystal glassware, Tiffany silverware, and the most adorable Tiffany tea sets.

This marked an *ah-ha!* moment for us. Toni had her wedding color: Tiffany's signature robin's-egg blue.

Is Tiffany blue a secret recipe? Is there a copyright on the color? The answer: yes. So I contacted Tiffany's VP of Creative Services for permission and a PMS chip of their blue for the eventual custom dyeing of the silk tablecloths, custom chair caps and chair pads, the carpet for the tent, and the thread used to embroider the initials *tLk* on white linen hemstitch napkins.

While reviewing my portfolio, Toni had taken a liking to the mirrored tabletops that showcased the frescoed ceilings of the ballroom where Lela Rochon and Antoine Fuqua hosted their reception. *What should Toni's tables reflect?* We looked at chandelier after chandelier. Nothing moved us. But her gown, with its crystal-beaded spaghetti-strap bodice, did.

Suspended above each table—twenty Austrian crystal strands of varying lengths. When lights from various points

Madison Avenue tells us that diamonds are a girl's best friend—but so are crystals.

above hit the crystals, the tent became a fairy-tale forest of diamonds, a sparkling wonderland.

How to cap such a magical evening?

Toni had shared with me her fondness for a particular scene in *My Best Friend's Wedding:* at the end of the reception, the couple is driven down a driveway lined with fireworks. *Hmm.* Why shouldn't a cherished silver-screen moment become Toni's reality? And so the Braxton-Lewis reception had as a finale "a booming and colorful fireworks display worthy of a major city's Fourth of July," one celebrity watcher later reported. It was the perfect ending to a fairy-tale day. And history can record that Toni Braxton's wedding day truly ended with a bang—a *Wow!*

A winter wonderland? A tropical expanse? How about a Moroccan palace? A savannah, perhaps? With a little initiative and ingenuity, almost any space can be transformed into whatever world you dare to dream. So before you start thinking about flowers, cake, and other elements of your wedding day, first meditate on the space and listen for the song.

Glamour should not only be seen but felt
in every room.

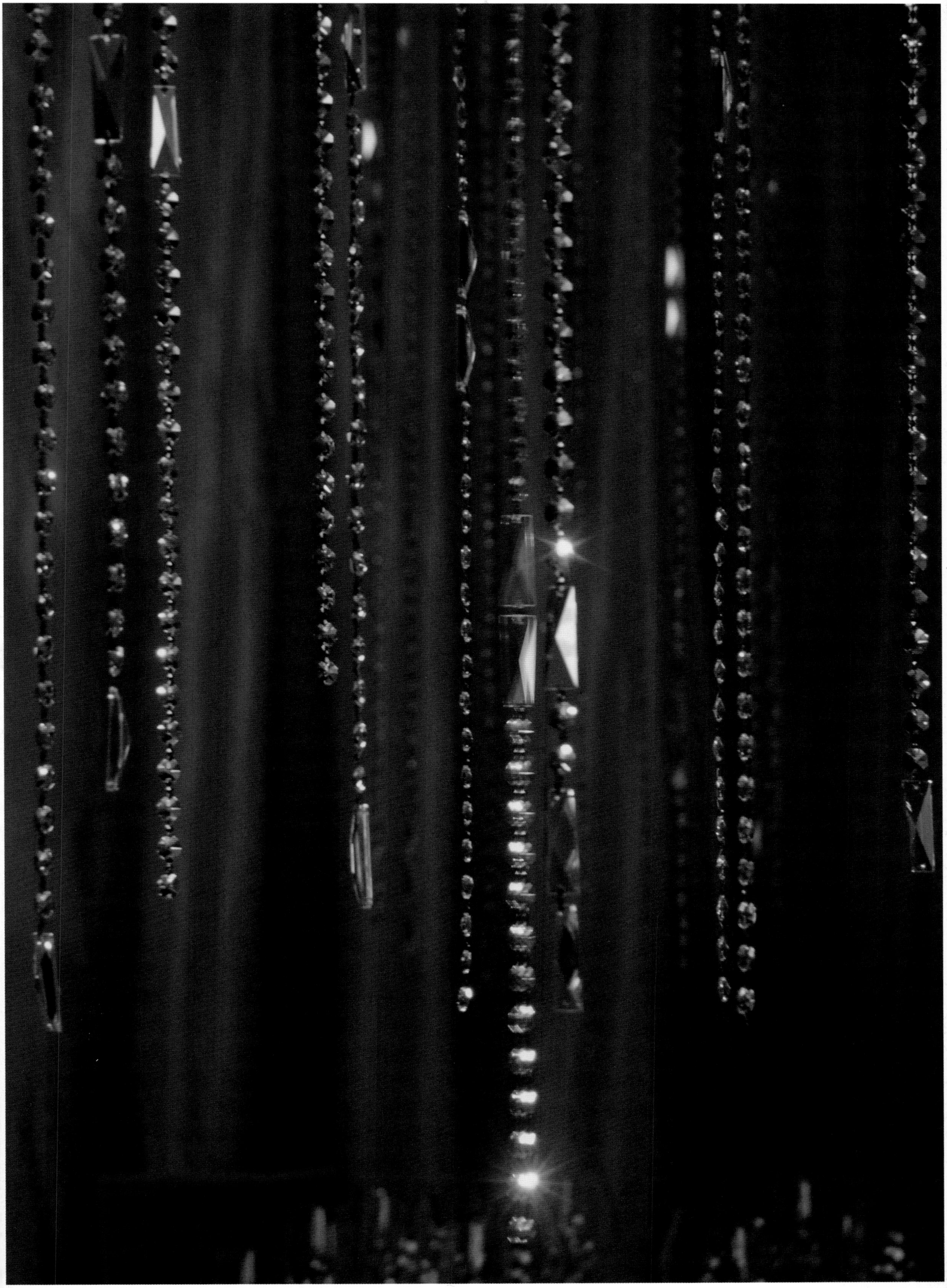

Oprah: How does the music come to you? Quincy Jones once told me that he can sometimes see melodies.

Bono: I've never seen the music. For me it's a puzzle. I hear strains of a melody, and only when I work it out to its end, can I be at peace. . . . [O]ne of the things that hits have and that great music always has . . . the music feels like it was already there.

—When I read this exchange in O *magazine, I thought,* That's what designing a space is like for me!

Before you start thinking about flowers, cake, and other elements of your wedding day, first meditate on the space and listen for the song.

Touches

There are many ways to give space verve and aura for a little or a lot of money. If recarpeting a ballroom is beyond your budget, envision what some strategically placed, thematic area rugs can do: floral- or foliage-infused if you want naturescape; Adinkra-patterned or Ndebele-styled if "roots"; abstract expressionism–inspired if your celebration carries a SoHo groove. If a couch or other seating in the site of your cocktail hour is a bit cold, toss in some soul with accent pillows.

Putting candles on windowsills and atop other surfaces (including guest tables) is a low-cost way to soften a room. Other varieties of a little light legerdemain can retone a room so well that major decorating is unnecessary. Smart lighting can mute a ballroom's garish carpet and make standard-issue white linens work just fine. Creative lighting can also hide ugly wallpaper, outdated curtains, and other blemishes.

Opposite: Several hundred hand-glued peacock feathers went into the making of this coverlet for the table at the entrance of a dining room where guests picked up their place cards.

Lighting a room amber, rose, or blue, for example, can imbue it with a completely new attitude. When a couple decided to use one tent for both the cocktail hour and the party, we lit the room blue for the former, red for the latter.

flora

Flowers are smiles, thank-yous, lush kisses. Like mountaintops and birdsong, they inspire reflection on creation. To borrow from Zora Neale Hurston, flowers are "a glance from God," as her character Janie said of her beloved in *Their Eyes Were Watching God*.

Dream with me a little while. Find a favorite flower and make it dance. What does it for you? The iris's regal serenity? The sunflower's pop? Oh-so-fragrant freesia's bounce? Or the calla lily's sleek grace and art deco echo? Hear the call to Eden and the earth primeval in the bird-of-paradise's "beak." See how the voluptuous peony (especially fuchsia) beckons, "Look at me and be sure to catch every angle." Tulips may be slight on scent, but check out their cool charm. For me, there is nothing more sublime and fine for all seasons than orchids. The green cymbidium is my personal favorite because it makes such a sexy, architectural statement.

Small flowers can make huge statements.
This cymbidium orchid is just one example.

No, I have not forgotten the flower we most associate with Eros: Lady Rose. Red, white, apricot, baby pink, mauve, light or deep yellow. Alba roses, Bourbon roses, giant Ecuadorian roses, damask, floribunda, black beauty, and on and on—in full bloom, still in the bud, long-stemmed. True, roses never go out of style, but I urge you not to shop for roses before you have explored the array of what Flora has to offer.

Dill, garlic, thyme, chives, and perhaps a pungent posy. Such went into some bridal bouquets of yore to ward off evil spirits. (Other combos allegedly ensured fertility.) Over time, bride after bride, with no interest in pagan practices, came to believe that a hand bouquet was yet another sine qua non for her wedding day. True, that hand-tied, nosegay, teardrop, or trailing bouquet can serve an important purpose: to combat the "spirit of nervous-ness," by giving the bride something with which to fidget.

Flowers seduced me at an early age. I learned the potency of their charms as they bewitched me with their vibrant colors and intoxicating scents. The ability of flowers to cast a spell on a room or enhance a special moment with their presence persuaded me to learn more about their subtle yet sublime powers. I love using flowers to express my fantasies and visions and dreams. They continually delight, surprise, fascinate, and mesmerize as they inspire me to create.

—Walter Hubert, *Silver Birches*

Don't let a florist buffalo you into run-of-the-mill bouquets.

Opposite: Black calla lilies offered great contrast to Sharhonda's all-white wedding gown.

If a hand bouquet works for you—maybe you will need something to occupy your hands—take care that your bouquet accents, and doesn't compete with, your gown. A fairy-tale wedding gown festooned with tulle, ribbons, and exquisite beading wants a simple, low-key bouquet, such as a pavé of French tulips or a tight ball of stephanotis. For your attendants, perhaps a smaller pavé of the flowers in your bouquet (same color or different). If you've chosen a modern, body-hugging dress, go dramatic. Imagine yourself with an arm sheaf of long-stemmed calla lilies and your attendants with pavés of mini calla lilies or other flowers, such as tulips or cymbidium orchids.

Above: For that indoor ceremony and reception, by all means let your florals do double duty. Following Sharhonda and Shawn's nuptials, with only minutes to spare, Walter moved the orchid halo under which they were married to the reception side of the ballroom where it framed their wedding cake.

Opposite: So maybe a floral wedding gown is a bit too risqué for you. How about a traditional gown with a peony bustle?

Allergies? You can still have a beautiful bouquet if you wish.

Prefer to keep your hands free? Consider a boa of peonies or dendrobium orchids, particularly if you will be wearing a gown. If you've got your eye on a midi, knee-length, or mini dress, how about a floral anklet? Make it cute (soft pink rose petals strung together), chic (a pavé of tulips), or unbelievably sexy (peonies). Another hands-free option is to wear flowers in your hair: a halo of stephanotis or a splash of gardenias or cattleya orchids on your best side. Or take a note from Kelis, who opted for a hand-painted gold headpiece of leaves and orchids.

For the other women of significance—your mother, your grandmother, his—I see no reason that their flowers have to coordinate with the wedding, especially as I don't think the mother of the bride and other mothers should look like members of the bridal party. Your color scheme may not suit them. Moreover, so much matchy-matchy is monoto-nous. Let their flowers suit their outfits. If you won't be certain until the eleventh hour what they will wear, choose from among those flowers that work with practically any-thing (calla lilies, gardenias, orchids, roses). Spare their clothes pinpricks by giving them wrist corsages. A tussy mussy is another option, as is flowers in their hair.

Boutonnières? Talk about tired. It's not the senior prom. How many men do you know—even the many who *love* flow-ers—who get excited about wearing flowers? Of course, if you give the guys boutonnières, they'll oblige because they know that women rule on wedding day. But why not allow them a comfort zone? There are other ways to make grooms, groomsmen, the father of the bride, and other fathers stand out. When hip-hop legend Nas married, he wore an ascot adorned with an antique African brooch his ladylove had given him just hours before.

Let your reception space determine whether flowers are in order, and if so, to what extent. A ballroom may benefit from clusters of pavé-style cymbidium orchids suspended from the ceiling, a water wall decked with calla lilies, or sim-ply a hand-painted dance floor to complement the carpet. A yacht party—why bother with flowers? If your feast takes place in a garden, no need to compete with Mother Nature.

Thinking of having hands-free bouquets? Consider something like this natural raffia backpack with copper silk straps and filled with chocolate cosmos (bridesmaid's dress not included).

The Center of Attention

Whether your centerpiece is composed of flowers or not, make sure it doesn't interfere with people's sight lines. Remember, too, that you will make a more powerful statement with, say, a single stem of dendrobium orchids than with a crowd of carnations or mums. This is not to say that you should reject out of hand common, inexpensive flowers. One of my favorite wedding flowers is the mophead hydrangea—not pricey at all. You can get big bang for the buck—and great beauty—if you choose from among the inexpensive posies those that are as striking as the hydrangea. The gerbera daisy is another example. Another tip: carnations and chrysanthemums are great for architecturally driven arrangements (in the shape of letters, for example).

In the mood for love.

Picture this: a strapless slender
silhouette with a boa like this.

in
sync
i live in music
—Ntozake Shange

chapter 4

We don't all boast the most fascinating sense of rhythm, but we all, as Ntozake Shange says, have a sound track to our lives. Music is deep calling to deep. Music *moods* us, from edgy to ecstatic. Adherents of the Mozart Effect® maintain that some sounds can strengthen our mental muscle and even heal.

For your wedding, ask, *How do I use music to move myself and everyone else to a particular zone? What sounds will keep my guests engaged—enthralled— from pre-ceremony to processional? From the first dance to the "That's all folks—we're off to Cap Juluca!"* Your goal is to be true to the spirit of the day, to orchestrate high-key, moment-to-moment flow and avoid disconnect, such as going from a Johnny Mathis classic to the latest hip-hop track.

If the last five weddings you attended featured a certain song, forget about it and get over it. Chances are that your guests have also heard that same song at wedding after wedding after . . . . While familiarity may not breed contempt, boredom is a distinct possibility. When it comes to your reception, no doubt about it, a tight party requires a great DJ who knows how to bring in the old-school with the hottest joints of the day. When it comes to key ceremonial moments, however, you do not want to be trite.

If, up to now, you have been attuned to only one groove—say, R&B—consider a change. Open up and expand your world of sound. You might find that a little country, jazz, salsa, or Gregorian chant in the mix might make your wedding all the more memorable and joyful.

There is nothing more romantic, more ethereal than live music, especially for the ceremony. When the wedding is in a space with astounding acoustics—*Wow!* Quantity isn't necessarily better when it comes to musicians. A forty-piece orchestra is great if you have it like that, but a quartet or even a solo musician (piano, flute, sax, cello, harp) may do just fine.

Everyone loves good lyrics, but there's a good case to be made for keeping the ceremony sounds instrumental. The spotlight should be on the bride. Instrumental music is less distracting. It also carries the thing that endears us to a song: rhythm and arrangement. If you are set on having a vocalist or two at the ceremony, consider that some songs are taken, as it were. Anyone who offers up, let's say, Patti LaBelle's "Have You Ever Loved Somebody" or Whitney's "The Greatest Love of All" and isn't Patti or Whitney is likely to disappoint and would do everyone a favor by choosing another song to make his or her own.

There's a great exception to every rule. When DeLeon Richards and Gary Sheffield renewed their vows in celebration of their one-year anniversary, their ceremony not only featured a choir, but CeCe Winans herself sang "For Always" during the communion. Yolanda Adams brought down the house with "That Name."

Gary knew that DeLeon would sing during the ceremony, but he had no idea that she had teamed up with her producer, Jerry Peters, on a new song, "Straight from the Heart," the title track of her next album.

Your celebration may be radically different. You may want classical music to carry the day. In that case, as your guests wait for the ceremony to commence, imagine them doing so to Handel's "Air." Imagine a trumpet fanfare announcing, *Here comes the groom!* The ladies-in-waiting and the groomsmen move easily up the aisle to Purcell's "Trumpet Voluntary" or something similar that is not superslow so as to spare attendants that awkward and outdated two-step.

When the groom and the attendants are in place, suddenly the orchestra breaks into the "Alleluia" portion of Mozart's "Exultate Jubilate" or Handel's "Arrival of the Queen of Sheba"—Toni Braxton's choice to signal her ascent to her darling. Then, with guests at attention, at the height of anticipation, the doors of the sanctuary open and you enter—not necessarily to "Here Comes the Bride," but instead, perhaps, to Pachelbel's "Canon."

After you have taken your vows, exchanged rings, been proclaimed husband and wife, and given yourselves over to that at-last, *at-last* kiss, arm in arm you two make your jubilant recessional to a sterling rendition of—not necessarily Beethoven's "Ode to Joy." Handel's equally uptempo "Royal Fireworks" and Widor's "Toccata" from the Fifth Symphony are among the universe of alternatives. You may decide not to walk down the aisle but—taking another tip from Toni Braxton—be swooped up in the arms of the groom.

Your day may be a softer shade of romantic, have a candlelight-and-violins vibe. The playlist for the reception might include some Sinatra and Sade. Or a more kick-it kind of energy might start you out on the right note.

When Sharhonda Jones and Boyz II Men's Shawn Stockman tied the knot, a ten-piece string section served up a prelude of R&B classics. The maid of honor and bridesmaids entered to a string rendition of "By Your Side." Shawn and his attendants stepped to Outkast's "So Fresh, So Clean." When came the bride . . .

Sharhonda chose to say no to Mendelssohn and yes to her man, with Boyz II Men's "I Do." She lip-synched along— "Do I promise you . . ."—as she glided up the aisle in her custom Tomasina gown with two dozen Schwarzwalder calla lilies in her hands.

For their recessional, Sharhonda and Shawn bounced to Stevie Wonder's "Every Beat of My Heart." Shawnee Simms and Jimmy Jackson had a similarly funky recessional: "Darlin' Darlin' Baby" by the O'Jays.

Opposite: Sharhonda lip-synchs "I Do" in a gorgeous gown with a basket-weave bodice and dropped-waist full skirt. Hundreds of Swarovski crystals infused into dozens of layers of tulle added a dynamic sparkle as she made her way to her man.

Below: It didn't take long for Shawn to trade in his formal kicks for his favorite pair of Adidas shell toes.

Opposite: Flower girls have their own good time at the Finney-Johnson reception in the Four Seasons Hotel in Beverly Hills. Center stage: "Little" Sara, the bride's niece.

Joe serenades Shawn and Sharhonda at their reception—and in the process woos all of the ladies.

Love is . . .

If it's a funky affair, how about skipping the reception
line—no heading to the head table. Instead, you newlyweds
should just hit the dance floor—*hard*, on something fast.
Have the MC signal guests to join in at the end of the first
song, then let any takers party hearty for two or three more
cuts. The tone of the party is set in the first three minutes
of your arrival. Good times do not just happen. They have to
be orchestrated, artfully arranged.

Make sure your DJ is in sync with your vision of the
day. Provide a clue on your desire to be creative and original by setting an example. Maybe Chaka Khan's "My
Funny Valentine" or Prince's "Adore" for the first dance?
Give your DJ a profile of your guests as well. Are most of
the attendees going to be under the age of thirty? Or
forty and up? Are they mostly socially liberal?
Conservative? A mix is more likely the reality. So variety
is always something I aspire to. But the tastes of the
couple should rule the day.

Nobody beats the Biz!

Love looks sooo

ooo good!

Love is...

A party-hearty reception may not be what you want. That's still no excuse to be boring and unmemorable. If you're devoutly religious, offer music appropriate for your belief.

Other ideas: Let your guests dine to a mime (children would love it), a stand-up comic with "family-hour" jokes, a dramatic performance piece, or a professional clown with a high-quality kit and caboodle of magic tricks.

The Looky Loo Party

flava!

chapter 5

The sea-salt-scented air on secluded Leeward Island of Anguilla was an invigorating reminder that we were a world away from the smog and congestion of L.A. The warm breeze was a luscious hello from heaven's mouth to Earth's ear.

Our D. R. Valentine design team had just deplaned a private jet with Shawnee Simms and her family. We were there to evaluate Anguilla's Cap Juluca, a five-star resort and spa on one of the purest beaches in the world. This idyllic spot was high on the list of possible venues for Shawnee's wedding. Due to a departure delay, we did not reach Anguilla until around midnight, but no problem for Cap Juluca's general manager, Eustace Guishard. He had returned from his home to greet us and to have the resort's open-air restaurant, Pimm's, "reawakened" so those of us who wanted to could have a bite to eat.

Just steps away from the most crystal blue water I had ever seen, Walter Hubert (art director), Peter Otero (set designer), and I feasted on selections from Pimm's Eurasian/Caribe cuisine: fresh mango gazpacho, fried plantains with a chile-lime sauce, herb-stuffed grouper with a drizzle of beurre blanc. *Is this real? Am I really here in this paradise— doing a site inspection? Oh, how blessed I am. . . . Thank you, Shawnee!* As I savored every morsel of the meal, I fell in love all over again with Caribbean dishes I had experienced as a child during travels with my mom.

My work has widened my appetites—opened me up to the vast varieties of cuisines. As memorable as that Cap Juluca "bite to eat" is a meal I had when my daughter and I,

sublime! Also on the table: white whole-kernel sweet polenta, butter-soft osso buco, angel hair pasta (*fatte in casa*) with organic summer vegetables (*in brodo*), and a sun-dried tomato and dry ricotta quiche. For dessert: a red currant tart with a short butter crust. It was the most amazing meal that I had during my vacation (which included gaining ten pounds from saying yes to too many pastries in Paris).

When your guests finish the meal, you want the melody to linger on.

while vacationing in Europe, met up with Walter Hubert and other friends in Florence to celebrate his birthday.

Walter's partner, Mark, had managed to secure reservations at Cibrèo (known to book three to four weeks in advance). And Mark, the top food connoisseur among us, did the ordering. Our spread included an item I would not have touched had I known what it was: tripe. But, oh, the *flava*! Its tang told me it had been treated for days to some marvelous marinade. Its sauce, a lemon-tomato coulis—so

Rounding out that sensational Cibrèo meal was a fabulous Florentine Chianti. For a nightcap, during our midnight stroll through the Piazza della Signoria, we delighted in gelato from Vivoli, one of Florence's premier *gelaterie*.

Nothing but the *best*! That's what you want for your wedding, most likely the grandest celebration of your life. The *best*, not necessarily the most expensive, but a feast with superior ingredients and preparation. When your guests finish the meal, you want the melody to linger on.

Are you considering one menu designed around a fish or meat entrée and another with vegetarians in mind? If you are, budget for extra of each entrée because inevitably a few people who said yes to Menu #1 on their response cards will change their minds when Menu #2 arrives and seems a bit more appetizing. If you know that only a handful of your guests are herbivores, go with one menu and have extra veggies on hand. Many vegetarians will be happy with a double salad—especially if that salad is fantastic!

Taking a Chance on Choice?

Take your pick . . . a tiny crab cake garnished with crème fraîche and slivers of red pepper, a cucumber round with tuna tartare sprinkled with sesame seeds and chives, or a bite-size caramelized onion tart topped with Fontina cheese and an asparagus tip.

Whether you choose to do one menu or two, a simple lunch (specialty soup, creative salad, raspberry sorbet), or a seven-course dinner replete with intermezzo, be very hands-on with the team commissioned to create probably the most memorable meal of your life. When you meet with a hotel or restaurant catering manager or a representative (or owner) of an independent catering company, let him or her know about the motif of your day. Then see what the place has to offer: review as many menus as they will show you. If you fall in love with the appetizer on Menu #1 and the entrée on Menu #7, ask them to mix and match. If a favorite dish is not among their standards or there's a particular recipe you would love to blend in, it cannot hurt to ask: "Instead of the baked trout, can you bake it and then sauté it in olive oil with capers and diced tomatoes?" or, "Instead of apple pie, can you make a thinly sliced apple tart topped with a scoop of homemade cinnamon ice cream drizzled with caramel sauce?" But be prepared for the results, because they may not get it as divinely perfect as celebrity chef Gerry Garvin does night after night at L.A.'s G. Garvin's Restaurant.

If none of their standards whets your appetite, and you have a good feeling about the establishment, ask if you can design your own menu. If so, ask for a meeting with the executive chef. Generally, anything is possible if you can handle the surcharges that special requests typically generate.

For that own-made menu, if you're not a culinary artist, take care to study up on the art of the menu. Basically, you want balance: not too much bland or too much spicy or too much tart or too much sweet. You might turn stomachs with a menu such as this: mesquite chicken breasts (smoked), curried basmati rice (spicy), gingered baby carrots (spicy/sweet), mesclun salad with basil-lime vinaigrette (tart), and assorted miniature cobblers (sweet/tart). You also want a menu that is not a bore color-wise (filet of sole, string beans almondine, scalloped potatoes, crème brûlée) or texturewise (herbed grilled salmon, yam-apple soufflé, creamed spinach).

This salad sings, "Spring is in the air!"

Below: Cornish hen with pomegranate glaze paired with cornbread stuffing and haricots verts with almond slivers.

Opposite: Marinated shrimp stacked between sugarcane bound with wilted scallions.

While you mull over menu possibilities, remember that, just as with flowers, there's a cost/in-season dynamic with many foods. And be discerning about what a caterer can deliver. Some dishes require a true culinary wizard. So if you're dreaming salmon, keep in mind that it takes some skill to serve it up succulent and full of flavor. Duck and veal are among the meats that can be a challenge to pull off successfully. If not properly marinated, lamb may come out

more gamey than you and your guests care for.

Pork? Not the best choice if you have one menu, because many people have sworn off pork for a variety of reasons. Beef? In an increasing number of households, beef is not what's for dinner. Perhaps you love shellfish—shrimp is generally a big crowd-pleaser. But unless you know all your guests very well, an all-shellfish menu might miscue: many people are allergic, some don't eat it for religious reasons, others never acquired the taste.

No wonder many brides play it safe and select chicken—pretty hard to wreck, a first choice for most meat eaters, and it's relatively inexpensive. Select a chicken dish your guests would rarely—if ever—make at home.

Once you have chosen your menu, you may wonder, *What will it look like?* When your guests look down upon their plates, they should behold a work of art. You want something that inspires—"This is too pretty to eat!"—as it tantalizes them to hurry up and taste. Ask for photographs of food presentations. If the samples are underwhelming, take some initiative.

Some establishments offer a tasting. Others won't unless you ask. If the answer is no, choose someone else. A tasting will give you some assurance—or signal that you need to go to a fallback plan, as happened with one of my clients.

April and LaShawn say yes, yes, yes! with
sparkling apple cider.

Several months before this client's wedding, I did a site inspection of her venue, a hotel. Along with making sure all of the logistical details were in order, my client and I did a taste test of the soul food menu she had so wanted. The tasting was a disaster.

The greens tasted like a bowl of salt. The smothered steak looked like a pile of brown lard on top of the plate. The mac and cheese was runny. The chicken was fried instead of baked, as requested. (I guess the chef got carried away with stereotype.) The peach cobbler had been made with canned peaches, and you could cut the cobbler with a knife and pick it up with a fork.

The chef looked to be about eighteen years old and had just graduated from culinary school. Not that there aren't young culinary geniuses, but this chef needed a lot more experience before he could venture into dishes not taught in school. Clearly, he did not have a clue as to what soul food is all about. Like other chefs I have encountered, he apparently thought it's all about salty or spicy versus *flavorful*. Rather than chance a second-time-around fiasco, my client decided to cut bait on our specialty menu and chose one of the hotel's standards.

When it comes to the service of the meal, my standard is sit-down. And it's personal. I love great service, love the idea of being served a meal rather than standing in what resembles a free-food line. When a client thinks buffet because she wants her party to have a relaxed vibe, I suggest a compromise: a plated dinner with a few optional action stations during the cocktail hour. So in addition to tray-passed items, we might also set up a pasta station with made-to-order pasta, a sushi bar, a mashed potato bar, and maybe a sizzling fajita bar. The client gets that touch of informality, and her guests have the pleasure of a sit-down dinner. It really is the ultimate way to dine, and so I say, let your guests experience that! After all, your wedding is the ultimate celebration of your life.

Table Talk

Chances are, the china that comes with your catering package will be fairly plain. It may also bear the signs of use after use after . . . . Wonderful food deserves wonderful surroundings. Rent a pattern that complements your theme. A fitting charger is such a lovely touch, and I say the charger should not be cleared until the dinner plate is (why deprive a table of some adornment?).

There's nothing like beautiful stemware to make a table shine and attractive flatware to make the dining experience more sublime. If a venue's china, stemware, and flatware are uninspired or downright ugly, rent more appealing tableware. It won't cost megabucks and may even be a savings in the long run. The tables are half the battle of a delectable room. Striking place settings can spare you the time and expense of redecorating a room. What's more, those standard-issue white linens may be A-OK, and a cluster of candles may be all the centerpiece you need.

crazy,

sexy,

cool.

chapter 6

chocolat?

The wedding cake, always a focal point in the room, usually sits on a specially designed table to draw all eyes. The wedding cake is the show-off. And I say, by all means, if it's fabulous, flaunt it!

To make it fabulous, bring your pastry chef of choice clippings or photos of elements that you think would look yummy on your cake. Don't limit your inspiration to photos of other wedding cakes. Your creative energy can come from a floral arrangement, a pair of great shoes, a beaded dress on a model strutting down a runway, a palatial estate, an exquisite piece of jewelry, a spray of precious gems, or your favorite children's story. Surrender to your fancies. That's the way to fully engage in creative exploration and begin to uncover ideas that you did not know you had.

And shape it your way. Have a tower of squares, circles, rectangles, diamonds, hexagons, octagons, or triangles. Or stray from pure geometry and make your cake a jazzy car, a dream house, a replica of your wedding dress, a musical instrument, a statue, or anything else your heart desires.

My goal is to create stunning wedding cakes that are actually worth eating. I want people to be bowled over by the presentation (be it simple and elegant or whimsical and fun or a masterpiece of edible art)—and dance in the street upon tasting!

Cake has always been nostalgic for me, as it was that special treat my grandmother gave me when I managed to behave myself. I assume that everyone has had a great cake in his or her lifetime, and I want to rekindle the memory of that experience when I consult with them about their wedding. To make cakes that are so ultragourmet that people cannot relate to them is an error in judgment by the pastry chef. Indeed, it can be excellent and down-home (whether home is Jersey City or Vienna) all at once.

—Sam Godfrey, *Perfect Endings*

The flavor options for wedding cakes are as extensive as the shape options. If you can conceive it, a baker can usually create it. When it comes to flavor and filling, take your pick: chocolate, lemon, strawberry, banana nut, cream cheese, Italian cream, lemon meringue, marble, key lime, peaches and cream, mango, mint chocolate chip, raspberry, chocolate ganache. The list goes on.

As for the icing on the cake, along with the very popular Italian buttercream, there's cream cheese, white chocolate,

milk chocolate, chocolate ganache. Fondant is the most popular finish for cakes with architectural elements. It leaves a very smooth and crisp finish to the top of the cake and is great for creating flowers and other toppings. But there's a downside: fondant is often thick and gummy. I have had some excellent fondant experiences—marvelously moist, eminently edible. But bakeries that can pull that off can be hard to find.

While mulling over style and substance possibilities, think of size, too. Instead of one grand cake that feeds two

Above: Nas and Kelis's red velvet and butter pound cake.

Opposite: What an absolute joy it was to work with Sylvia Weinstock on April and LaShawn's chocolate cake, which was gilded in edible gold and patterned with the embroidered design from April's gown.

Above: Sierra chose a cake echoing gift boxes in remembrance of all the surprises Keary had showered upon her during their courtship. And the surprises kept coming: Keary arranged for Kenny Lattimore and Chanté Moore to serenade Sierra at the reception.

The groom's cake is an old southern custom: traditionally red velvet and in the shape of an animal. (Remember the red velvet armadillo groom's cake in *Steel Magnolias*?) I say, when it comes to the groom's cake, you should be guided by what's at the heart of the matter: the groom's cake is a way to tell your man that this day is also about him. Elegant Cheesecakes in Atlanta, Georgia, created the perfect groom's cake for Jimmy Jackson, one that clearly reflected his favorite pastime.

hundred, have two hundred miniature, custom-designed wedding cakes. For a casual afternoon affair, go cupcake.

Thinking about placing those plastic or ceramic folks atop your cake? Please, think again. You could spoil your cake with Mr. and Mrs. Stilted. Even if you can find lifelike ones that do justice to black people, you don't have to go there simply because it's tradition. If your cake calls for a topper, think more along the lines of flowers, a crystal hummingbird, or a symbol that holds some significance for you. And if you'd rather spend the extra money on those beaded place cards, you can always order a small wedding cake designed to your liking and then subsidize the servings with a couple of sheet cakes precut in the kitchen and served to guests after you have cut your cake.

When advising clients, I am indebted to pastry chef Sam Godfrey for much of my take on wedding cakes. Sam possesses the kind of right-on sensibilities you should seek in your cake maker. Like the best pastry chefs, Sam is a purist. At the outset of his career, he decided to bake absolutely from scratch, "nothing pre-made from a bag, box, or can." Sam insists on high-quality ingredients—"the best chocolate, butter, cream, and liqueurs that I can find. Merely choosing butter over Crisco was not enough . . . I want the *best* butter." Another of Sam's tenets to bake by is to work with Mother Nature: for example, he will use strawberries only when they are in season.

And Sam prefers to work with a bride only after she has planned her menu. "Only after you have selected your meal will you truly know what you will crave for dessert," he explains. "If you have feasted on a substantial multicourse meal, a huge slice of carrot cake is most likely not very appealing. But a light and airy butter cake, filled with a refreshingly tangy organic lemon mousse and vine-ripened berries, might hit the spot. Conversely, if you have dined on delicate fare, an ultrarich, serious chocolate caramel cake will do just fine!"

Do You Have to Serve Cake?

In these calorie- and carb-counting, diabetes-on-the-rise times, you may want to defy tradition by having no wedding cake at all. Have a dazzling dessert bar instead. Make it one that will make everyone happy—mix it up with fresh fruit sorbet, soy ice cream, wheat-free brownies, flourless chocolate cake, wheat-free cookies made with honey, fresh fruit with whipped cream, a smoothie bar, frozen grapes or strawberries topped with Grand Marnier. By the way, if you simply can't fight the feeling of your addiction to chocolate, call on Dylan's Candy Bar to design a custom candy bar to your taste, just as they did for Nas and Kelis.

the
WOW!

After you, that is.

Give yourselves and your loved ones that something extra. Make the day pop—and maybe even move people to tears—when your guests least expect it. The *Wow!* might be stunningly original vows. LaShawn Daniels, in his vows, referred to April Brown as the "bangingest" track he had ever produced and the most beautiful love song he had ever written, fitting for a music producer.

Your guests are sure to take notice if you put a fresh spin on the bridal bouquet toss (another holdover from the days of yore, when a bride made the toss to a bevy of barely postpubescent maidens). The cattle call to pounce for the bridal bouquet will inevitably make those already uncomfortable about their singleness more uncomfortable. Plus, the desperate (and obviously superstitious) women are apt to make fools of themselves—showing their unmentionables in their leaps, knocking down others in their grabs, and perhaps ripping panty hose, skinning knees.

Pages 164 and 165: The silver and
brass bells that greeted Lela and
Antoine's guests at the church.

Television producer Sara Finney had a very dignified and memorable bridal-bouquet moment. Near the end of the reception, the MC asked married couples to take the dance floor. After a few minutes, he announced, "Anyone married less than a day, please take your seat." Sara and her husband, Robert, of course, were the only couple to leave. After another little while—"Anyone married five years or less" . . . Then, "Anyone married twenty years or less."

After "sixty years or less," one couple remained on the dance floor. Everyone could see how deeply in love those seniors still were: from the way he rubbed her back as they slow-danced, the way she constantly smiled at him, the way they sure did look alike.

As the music faded, Sara returned to the dance floor. "I've got something special for you," she said to the woman. "I want you to have my bouquet, but I don't want to throw it. I want to give it to you, for being such a role model and demonstrating to us all that love can last." Like original vows, that was a *Wow!*—and truly sacred moment—that cost nothing.

Mango calla lilies spell "C" for Sierra and Keary Colbert.

You may not want any man but your husband to touch a garter that has touched your thigh. You may even want to tell your guests the reason for your decision to forgo the garter toss. That may very well elicit a *Wow!* from some folks, and certainly a *Whew!* from most of the single fellas who get corralled for the toss and who often choose to be too cool, as in, *I ain't looking to get married no time soon!* Most just stand there refusing to reach for the garter, content to let it glance upside some unlucky dude's head and flop to the floor.

The *Wow!* for one of my first big-budget productions in Oakland carried a nominal cost. I had the couple's favorite portrait from their engagement photo shoot enlarged, affixed to foam core, and displayed on an easel at the entrance of the members-only club where they hosted their reception. On hand at the easel were several gold-paint pens for guests to sign and write well wishes. Far more memorable and meaningful than a guest book.

Another low-cost *Wow!* is to name guest tables along with numbering them. Work with a concept such as "Love Is . . . ," with each table completing the sentence. Table 2 might be "Awesome," table 3 "Sexy," and others "Expensive," "Mind-blowing," "Heaven-sent."

Sharhonda Jones and Shawn Stockman were game for a lot of *Wow!* Their first one started two days before the wedding, on the Thursday night when about one hundred people (attendants and guests) checked into the Wyndham

Hotel in Toledo, Ohio, Sharhonda's hometown. In each room, I had a bottle of Fiji water and two crystal water goblets placed at bedside, and propped up against the pillows, a message on a small card.

Sharhonda and Shawn's entire affair took place in the Wyndham ballroom. We transformed part of the ballroom into a wedding chapel. Another part was readorned for dining and dancing—with a one-of-a-kind aquarium dance floor that elicited many a *Wow!*

While guests dined and danced, they had no idea that, behind the curtained wall where the ceremony had taken place, Walter Hubert was calling the shots as crews were swiftly working to shift the space into a full-action casino where guests would be able to play blackjack, roulette, craps, and slot machines. After the waitstaff had cleared entrées from tables and on cue to R. Kelly and Keith Murray's "Home Alone," the curtain parted to reveal the casino. "It's gonna be a party, y'all!" Biz Markie assured the crowd.

From sterling silver trays, the waitstaff served guests baby blue velvet pouches of gold-plated, monogrammed casino chips. One by one, table by table, guests went gaming. The chips had no monetary value. People played for points. The endgame was prizes for the lucky three who racked up the most points. First prize was a DVD player; second, a cell phone; third, a Palm Pilot, newly the rage at the time.

Men always want to be a woman's first love; women have a more subtle instinct: what they like is to be a man's last romance.

Shawnee Simms and Jimmy Jackson's *Wows!* started the morning of the wedding, for guests and attendants occupying 150 rooms at Atlanta's Ritz-Carlton in Buckhead. The night before, I pulled an all-nighter recording a personalized wake-up call for each room at my perkiest even at 3 A.M.

Good morning, Mr. and Mrs. Masters. This is Diann Valentine, Shawnee and Jimmy's wedding producer. They wanted me to call and say good morning on their behalf. Also, they wanted me to tell you to make sure you allot plenty of time to prepare for the celebration. You don't want to be late, because I promise you this will be the most beautiful wedding experience you've ever had.

That gesture cost only about three hundred dollars. (The tough part was getting the in-house technicians to cease trying to convince me that what I wanted to do was impossible. It's amazing what you can get out of people when you refuse to take no for an answer.)

When Shawnee and Jimmy's guests arrived at Wieuca Road Baptist Church, they were greeted by four harpists on white platforms in the sanctuary foyer. After the ceremony, guests were gently (but quickly!) ushered from the church and asked to remain outside while Shawnee and Jimmy had their photo session. Each guest received a ballet pink organza sachet filled with pink rose petals. Remember, this was Atlanta—in July. Even at seven o'clock in the evening, it had

Opposite: Sharhonda's flower girls carried these crystal-banded baby blue gift boxes filled with white rose petals.

Below: Down to the place card holders for the bridal party, Shawnee spared no expense when it came to infusing her and Jimmy's personalities into every aspect of their celebration.

to have been at least one hundred degrees. To keep the guests from wilting, we tray-passed chilled towels that had been dipped in rose water, so people could dab their pulse points. We followed that up with highball glasses of sparkling pink lemonade garnished with an edible pink rose petal.

When Shawnee and Jimmy emerged from the church, the crowd of roughly five hundred literally *rose* to the occasion. (I advise against throwing rose petals for the bride's processional and the couple's recessional. With some carpeting and runners, it is a recipe for a slip-and-fall.)

Shawnee and Jimmy also wowed the crowd with the way they traveled to the reception at the Ritz-Carlton: in a princess carriage, drawn by two Black Beauty show horses. At the head of the procession were four members of the Morehouse College marching band, all decked out in toy-soldier costumes. Bringing up the rear were pairs of bridal attendants, two by two, in black Lincoln Town Cars. Potential problems with impatient drivers? Yes, I'd thought of that. I obtained a lane closure permit to cease traffic on two lanes of Peachtree Road for the two miles from the church to the Ritz-Carlton. I had also arranged for a motorcycle cop escort.

The final *Wow!* of the Simms-Jackson celebration came at the tail end of the reception: Shawnee's something-extra for Jimmy, a cigar connoisseur. In a room across from the main dining room, we created a cigar lounge. As the dining and dancing waned, Jimmy and other dreamboats (and a woman or two) retired to the lounge to enjoy a cigar hand-rolled on the spot by a bona fide *torcedor*, eat groom's cake, or sip a top-shelf Cognac (Louis XIII)—or do all three.

To wow her chocoholic husband, April Brown wanted a chocolate bar on top of a huge chocolate wedding cake. Her wish was my command—happily, and with no half-stepping. *Why not have the milk chocolate morsels tailor-made for April and LaShawn?* She had been a hairstylist, and so there were miniature chocolate combs, brushes, scissors, hair dryers, and hairspray cans. Given his profession—chocolate CDs, pens, computers, and musical notes.

Daydreaming on your *Wow!* may be the springboard to the design of your entire day. Or you may want to hold off until you have all your basics mapped out. Then again, you may want to pack all the *Wow!* into your attire.

The days of netting and candied almonds are over. (Please, do not bring them back.) If you offer your guests a *Wow!*, it or some element of it can double as a favor. Bear in mind, too, that many people will make the invitation, their place cards, or the menu their souvenir.

Should you choose to do a favor, let it be something that is both practical and fabulous—as in unique, clever, *different.* Otherwise, it will be in the trash can by midnight. Money wasted.

Forget the Favors?

Opposite: The roulette wheel got plenty of action at Shawn and Sharhonda's casino.

the call to
attend

chapter 8

"I have found him!" That's what you are announcing. So make your invitation ensemble a magnificent statement about your love and where you are in life. Your invitation might also carry a glimpse of how you and Mr. Right came together or a highlight from the moment you said "Yes!" While you're at it, clue your guests in on the kind of experience they can expect. A-N-T-I-C-I-P-A-T-I-O-N . . .

Don't be afraid of color. The idea that black type on white (or ecru) signals class is, well, living by someone else's rules.

There are so many things that make life worthwhile
Good friends, family and hopes all make me smile
Yet you wish for something impossible and new
You hope maybe someday it will all come true.

I have one dream that always remains the same
Boyz II Men is his fame, and Shawn is his name
My life would be great, even if we just date
I don't mind, that's fine, I will leave it up to fate...

Jones/Stockman Wedding
c/o D.R. Valentine & Associates
137 North Larchmont Boulevard Number
Los Angeles, California
9 0 0 0 4

Kindly respond by

What makes for a class act is not the color of the paper, but its quality: twenty-eight pound or heavier. Dream papers include rice paper and those composed of 100 percent rag. There are also handmade papers infused with botanicals or intertwined with fine gold threads, deckle-edged paper with hand-painted borders in rich metallic tones, an assortment of stunning vellums or "translucents," and a dazzling array of thirty-two-pound "opalescent" metallics. For some of the most beautiful imported papers, look to Italy and Japan.

That surprise element of glitter, confetti, flower petals, and such inside invitations is just too cute for a child's birthday party. But for your wedding? Such stuff often annoys grown-ups because of the mess it makes on desks or floors. It can spoil your *ah-ha!* moment.

As for typeface, it certainly does not have to be a carnival of curlicue if that is not you. But if your celebration is

Euro royal, by all means a very swirled script would nicely complement that. On the other hand, if your theme is more minimalist, something sans serif would be a good match.

And whose call to attend is it anyway? Traditionally, whoever is hosting the celebration. With many of today's couples paying for their celebrations, we see more and more invitations that read something like this:

> Marilyn Lockwood and Stephen Cobb
>
> invite you to share in the celebration of their love
>
> on Saturday, the thirteenth day of March,
>
> Two Thousand and six
>
> at six o'clock in the evening
>
> First Baptist Church
>
> Los Angeles, California

If the couple's reception will be at a different location, the reception card might read:

FOOD,
FESTIVITIES,
AND A **FUNKY GOOD TIME**

Immediately following the ceremony
W Hotel
930 Hilgard Avenue
Los Angeles, California

But, I say, if the only reason that you and your beloved are paying for the event is because you can more easily afford to do so than your parents, why not give your parents the honor of being the titular hosts? If your parents have waited all their lives for this, if they have invested some twenty or more years of TLC (and money) in you, that is the least you can do. Hence:

Mr. and Mrs. Matthew Lockwood
invite you to share in their happiness as their daughter

Marilyn Lockwood

and

Stephen Cobb

are united in love

on . . .

(Your stationer can advise you on the etiquette of handling complicated situations, for example, if your parents are divorced and remarried or divorced and not remarried.)

There is a reason that, in these examples, I did not offer up "request the honor of your presence." That's fine if you're a Victorian kinda gal. If you aren't . . . your wedding, your words. Be as down-home, jazzy, or whimsical as you want to be, just so long as you provide the essential three *W*s—Who, When, Where—and just so long as your call to attend complements the tone and tempo of your celebration.

Most of your guests will assume dressy attire unless otherwise advised. Still, it never hurts to encourage them in the direction you want them to go, as one of my clients did with this invitation:

> Praise God from Whom All Blessings Flow!
>
> Sara Vernetta Finney
>
> and
>
> Robert Lee Johnson, Jr.
>
> Invite you to join in their celebration as they
>
> "Tell it to the preacher"
>
> Before family, friends and the Good Lord!
>
> On Sunday, the ninth of June
>
> Two thousand two
>
> At four o'clock in the afternoon . . .
>
> Reception immediately following
>
> Fabulous attire

Your call to attend announces the start of a new chapter in your life, so handle that call with care.

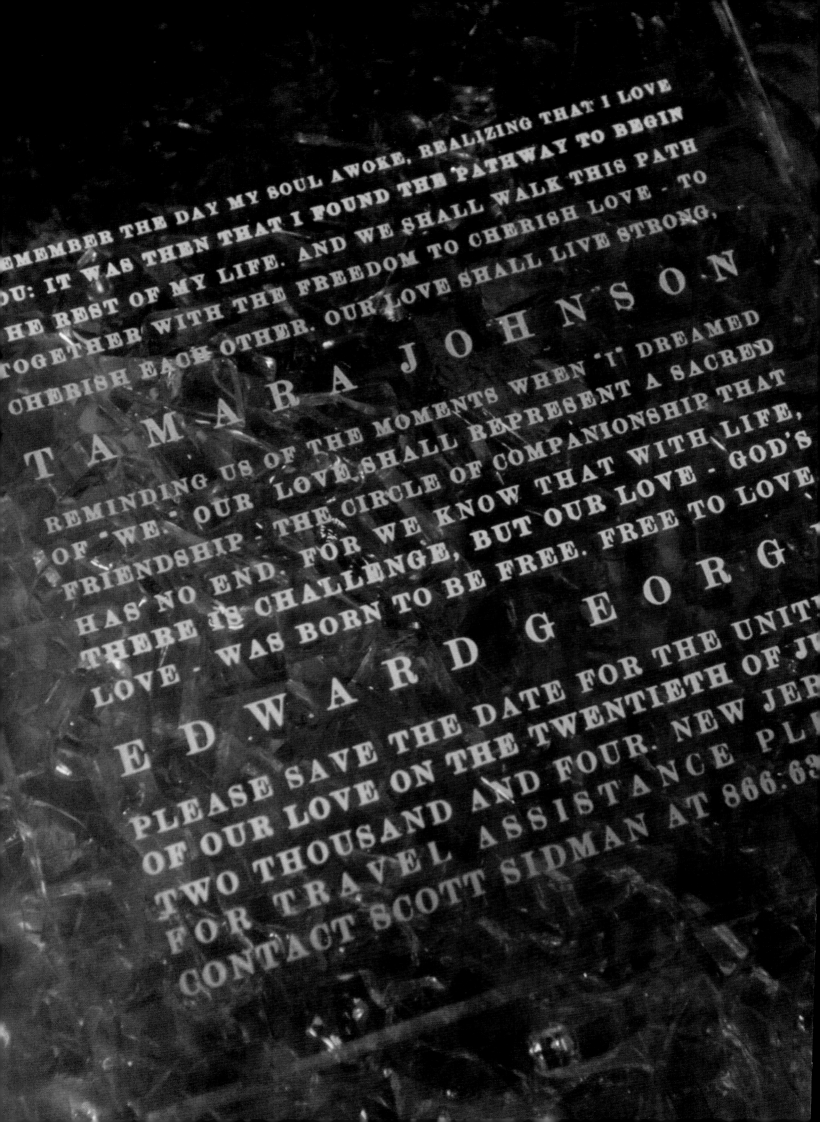

[REM]EMBER THE DAY MY SOUL AWOKE, REALIZING THAT I LOVE [Y]OU: IT WAS THEN THAT I FOUND THE PATHWAY TO BEGIN [T]HE REST OF MY LIFE. AND WE SHALL WALK THIS PATH TOGETHER WITH THE FREEDOM TO CHERISH LOVE - TO CHERISH EACH OTHER. OUR LOVE SHALL LIVE STRONG,

TAMARA JOHNSON

REMINDING US OF THE MOMENTS WHEN "I" DREAMED OF "WE". OUR LOVE SHALL REPRESENT A SACRED FRIENDSHIP - THE CIRCLE OF COMPANIONSHIP THAT HAS NO END. FOR WE KNOW THAT WITH LIFE, THERE IS CHALLENGE, BUT OUR LOVE - GOD'S LOVE - WAS BORN TO BE FREE. FREE TO LOVE.

EDWARD GEORG[E]

PLEASE SAVE THE DATE FOR THE UNIT[ING] OF OUR LOVE ON THE TWENTIETH OF JU[NE] TWO THOUSAND AND FOUR. NEW JE[RSEY] FOR TRAVEL ASSISTANCE PL[EASE] CONTACT SCOTT SIDMAN AT 866.63[...]

Save the Date!

Save-the-dates are quite common with my clients, as many of them are planning out-of-state weddings with guest lists that span the globe. If yours will include many people who live far away or are globe-trotters, save-the-date cards make sense. If you truly want long-distancers to attend your glory day, give them ample time to make travel arrangements.

A save-the-date card may even be a teaser, giving guests a first glimpse of the celebration and getting them excited and eager to attend. I also like to use the save-the-date to give guests a little insight into a couple's relationship. Poetry . . . Make it personal—it's supposed to be.

chapter 9

click!

The candles have burned down, all the food and drink has been consumed, and that cacophony of "Congratulations!" is a whisper in the wind. What's left?

Your canvas of memories. A wedding album and a videotape are more than nice souvenirs. They're about documenting a milestone, keeping history. If you and your love plan to have children, they are also about starting your family archives. When it comes to cost-cutting, two elements that I say never, ever, skimp on: your gown and the record of your precious memories.

Some traditions never lose their allure as Sierra and Keary Colbert, friends since childhood, bear witness.

Ideally, documenting the climax of your forever-and-a-day romance should not be limited to the *during*. Have a cornucopia of before and after shots. Perhaps the tape begins to roll at the rehearsal dinner. And the this-is-your-life resumes on the morning of and continues through the rest of the day, up until the moment that you and your husband spirit away for some greatly anticipated privacy.

Sara and Robert step into their new beginning.

Between the prelude and coda of your celebration, you want candid photos of the people who showed up to love you and rejoice. You want shots of details that made the difference, such as Sharhonda and Shawn's aquarium dance floor (which almost gave me gray hair); Shawnee and Jimmy's horse-drawn princess carriage (brought in all the way from New York); and the custom copper chair place cards that April Brown (and I) could not live without. Also worth preserving, the symbols and signposts along the way.

Grace and style never grow old.

Looks like little Manny has pledged to love and honor (and obey?) Sharhonda's flower girl, Taylor.

SECOND NEWS

THE BLADE · TOLEDO, OHIO ■ SATURDAY, SEPTEMBER 1, 2001

SECTION B · PAGE 1

SUPPORT TOLEDO'S EAST

Toledo schools accept Marina financing plan

BUSINESS
UAW might get 2nd vote at hospital
Page 9

City site of celebrity wedding

Boyz II Men star to become married man in Toledo

Health of Toledo schools a concern for candidates

ELECTION 2001

CRIME WATCH

WEATHER REPORT

INSIDE

Wow, look how far you have traveled for us.
We thank you from the bottom of our hearts.
We hope that you will enjoy this
weekend as much as we will!
Love, Shawn and Sharhonda

Schedule of Events
The Wedding Ceremony
Saturday, September 1st
The Wedding will start promptly at 4:00 p.m.

The Sunday Brunch
Sunday, September 2nd
11:00 a.m.
The Ashley Room
The Wyndham Toledo

In your search for a photographer and videographer, seek true artists with a passion for capturing reflections and reverberations of love. Just like with your man, when the right one comes along, you'll know—the minute you see his or her work.

Opposite: Instead of bouquets, boxes, or baskets, Shawnee's flower girls walked up the aisle with a floral rope.

If you have a large guest list (over two hundred people), ideally you want two photographers: the primary to shadow you, the number two to focus on your guests.

Your photographer(s) should be as adept at candids as at portraiture, able to be a fly on the wall scanning the scene and zeroing in on *ah-ha*, precious, or wacky moments: a tear tracking down a father's cheek; the groom in an "I'm ready, willing, and able" stance; Great-Aunt Jessie tapping her cane to "Them Their Eyes."

In spying a magic moment and making that split-second decision to *click*, the photographer knows to keep snapping five, eight, ten, or more frames of the same moment to get that money shot. You deserve images that leave you speech-less, tearful, and perhaps even scratching your head—*When did he get that shot?*—and amazed—*I never even noticed that!*

For portraiture, the photographer must be able to do more than tell everyone when to say "guacamole." You want someone who can arrange a portrait in such a way that the finished product looks like a candid.

The Portrait Police

For that postceremony photo session, have at least one Portrait Police. When a wedding takes place in a church, for example, after the recessional the Portrait Police sees to it that the bride and groom are whisked away to a nearby "safe room." The Portrait Police makes sure guests leave the church with dispatch—everybody except for the nears-and-dears who are to be in the photography session. Now the hard part.

The Portrait Police must also get your nears-and-dears not to whip out their own cameras while the photographer is shooting; otherwise, your would-be precious memories could end up overexposed because of their flashes. Problem number two: If your nears-and-dears are obedient and show restraint, if you allow them to get their shots after the photographer has wrapped, your photo session will take for . . . ever. You and everybody else may get cranky—including your guests who are downstairs, a few blocks away, or across town waiting for the reception to commence. The ideal? Let the Portrait Police announce that after the photographer is done, everyone else can have ten minutes of picture-taking time.

When you interview a photographer, inquire about your options when it comes to the final product. Look at a photographer's glossy and matte work and think about which finish you prefer. Ask questions. Will the images be on paper that will last a millennium? Is hand-printing an option so the photographs look all the more like works of art? What about development on canvas?

I advise against one-stop shopping when it comes to your photographer and videographer. With package deals, one is probably riding on the other's coattail. So the photographer may be an ace, but his cousin Willie's sole talent is a steady hand.

Know what your options are when it comes to the videographer's stock. Super VHS? Digital? Beta or Digibeta for super-crisp quality? If shot in 16mm, your video will be more akin to a film, because 16mm allows for more flexibility—and hence, creativity—in the editing room. Find out, too, whether a videographer has state-of-the-art equipment to capture a close-up from one hundred feet away. If not, you'll have to contend with an up-close and way-too-personal camera in your face.

How many cameras? One? Three? Consider the difference between the final cut of a one-camera film, such as *The Blair Witch Project,* and an episode of your favorite sitcom and scenes from an action-packed film such as *Training Day.*

When you review a videographer's work, look for clean cuts, smooth transitions from frame to frame, and seamless shifts from color to black-and-white to sepia. The more of a videographer's highlight reels you sample, the sharper your eye will become, the more your gut will guide. Too, you can always rely on the expertise of your wedding planner.

If a videographer or photographer has a penchant for special effects (strobes, explosions), say, "Thanks so much for your time," and move on. On anniversaries to come, you will want to flip through an album of timeless beauty, amazing grace. When you go to the videotape, you will not want to cringe—*What in the world were we thinking?*

Photographers and videographers know the standards: the vows, the kiss, the recessional, the first dance, the cutting of the cake. They know to get portraits of the bride and groom, the bridal party, parents, et cetera, et cetera. They know a lot. Still, don't let them tell you, "I know what to do," and leave it at that—unless they know *you:* know that you would love a shot of your first-light, tea-and-toast breakfast with Grandma, a portrait of all the elders in your clan, a shot of your mother praying for you before the festivities commence; and a cockeyed shot of you at the end of the day kicking off those jewel-studded Roberto Cavallis.

Even when I am dealing with true artists, I often storyboard the day to ensure that they will plot the course my client wants and to get their creative juices flowing.

Store the negatives from your wedding photos and your video master in a safe-deposit box. You may also want to store other mementos from your day: a copy of your invitation ensemble and other paperware, such as a menu. Take care to keep any one-of-a-kind mementos, as April Brown did when she had framed the several pages of Gucci notepaper on which LaShawn Daniels penned his vows.

I have never been that keen on freezing a slice of wedding cake, because the cake tastes terrible after a year. Where's the pleasure? I am, however, a sucker for the preservation of the wedding dress (cleaned, then sealed in an airtight box).

For Keeps

see (and be)

no evil

Throw a Pamper Party! A week before Shawnee Simms wed Jimmy Jackson, she had a spa date. So did her twelve brides-maids. So did several other women dear to her and to them.

For Shawnee's Pamper Party, we bought out an entire day at an exclusive day spa in Atlanta, Georgia, the destination city for Shawnee's fairy-tale wedding. One luxury shuttle bus cruised Shawnee and company to their spa experience, while another one carried her beloved and his crew to a golf outing.

At the spa, Shawnee and her guests had the pleasure of a full-body massage, manicure, pedicure, and foot massage, and aromatherapy breathing exercises. What's more, Shawnee gave each woman a pair of cotton poplin, pink heart pajamas from my sleepwear collection and a pair of pink cashmere slippers. Lunch and mimosas were catered in for this girls'-day-out moment of paradise. Bodies were beautified, spirits uplifted.

In her common spirit of generosity, Shawnee had not only thanked the women for celebrating with her but also ensured that they would be forgiving and understanding of any demands she might make as her celebratory weekend approached. Equally important, Shawnee had given herself a megadose of de-stress.

No matter how excellent and fine-tuned the planning, no matter if money is no object, no matter if you have not one quiver of doubt that your man is your everlasting love, no matter how smoothly everything has gone—as your wedding day approaches, you will be stressed. You may even start borrowing trouble: *What if it rains? What if I rip my wedding dress while I'm putting it on? What if the bakery has an accident and my wedding cake is ruined?*

Indeed, all may not go smoothly. A bridesmaid might cancel a month before the wedding. Your caterer might close up shop. The printer could goof on your invitations. Do *everybody* a favor—most of all yourself! De-stress and rejuvenate so that you do not end up one evil so-and-so and a face-all-broke-out bride.

Derrick Rutledge—
"The Makeup Maestro."

In Indonesia, the bride-to-be enjoys a Javanese royal lulur ritual, conducted each day for forty days before her wedding to get her prepared for the ceremony. During this time, she is given a Balinese massage, a sweet skin scrub, and a full-body mask with yogurt, turmeric, rice, and jasmine essential oil. She is also treated to flower-petal baths.

The older female relatives who administer the lulur also use the time to pass on wisdom and nurturing. And it is also believed that the more relaxed the bride, the more likely she is to conceive on the wedding night.

—Nina Curtis, The Nile Institute

Wedding or not, if you live in or near Beverly Hills or are planning a visit, treat yourself to The Nile Institute's wonders. Nina, "Spa Diva," is known for her butterfly fingers, which always put me right to sleep during my facials. Plus, she always ends each visit with a neck and shoulder massage. Considering that this is where I hold all of my stress, it is like a few minutes of paradise.

Give yourself a getaway. If you want a great-outdoors, truly mountaintop experience, seek out a place like Ten Thousand Waves, a Japanese health spa in Santa Fe, New Mexico. There, you can opt for an outdoor hot tub and indulge in holistic head-to-toe treatments (from a Yasuragi hair-and-scalp to an Amma hand-and-foot massage).

For a more tropical-island atmosphere, check into a pampering palace like Miami's Spa at the Mandarin Oriental on Brickell Key, where you can book a room (a suite, actually) with a soul-stirring view: three-quarters of the room has wraparound windows, allowing you a grand look at the ocean's ice blue waves. (The best hot-rock massage I ever had was at that Mandarin.)

If a top-of-the-line, full-out spa experience is not an option but a mini one is, let it be at a true spa—Jacuzzi, showers, changing rooms, blow dryers, and a panoply of first-class services. Some places posing as spas are little more than slightly souped-up nail salons. They call a closet a massage room.

If you can manage only one or two pre–wedding day treats, make one of them a full-body aromatherapy massage (lavender, gardenia, and jasmine are among the calming scents). Consider, too, dispelling nervous tension and getting a nervous system tune-up with a hand-and-foot reflexology session. For some, the best bodywork will be a visit to an acupuncturist or chiropractor. If nothing else, along with getting your hair and nails done the day before or the day of the wedding, get a major facial a week before.

Your stress-release regimen could be something as simple as afternoon tea at the poshest hotel in town or an overnight at a nice hotel if you don't live solo and need some time alone. A day at an arboretum or a botanical garden might also do you a world of good.

Your serenity bath may be your daily quiet time: a time to pray, say your affirmations, thank God for your blessings, or do whatever you do to reach balance.

At home, take advantage of one of the most therapeutic elements on the planet—something that is literally at your fingertips: water. Take a long bath several nights—if not every night—during the countdown week. For maximum moisturizing, make it one with a couple of gallons of heated whole milk and several dollops of honey. Or stick with your tried-and-true bath salts or gel. Soak in the air of scented candles or the essence of a few strands of gardenia. Play a soothing song, turn on your mini serenity fountain, or tune your satellite radio to the sound of a babbling brook or a rain-forest rhapsody. Or perhaps the only sound you need is silence.

Your serenity bath may be your daily quiet time: a time to pray, say your affirmations, thank God for your blessings, or do whatever you do to reach balance. If it's not already a part of your program, give yourself fifteen to thirty minutes a day of quiet time those last seven days. And check out the anxiety-defying effects of various breathing techniques. And a fast walk.

If You Must

Need to shed some pounds? Don't hang your hopes on an eleventh-hour crash diet. Start a diet-and-exercise regime (or up the ante on your current one) at least six months before the wedding.

After you say "I do," don't dive back into the M&M's! Many women make the mistake of doing things for the wedding that they do not intend to maintain for the marriage, setting themselves up for the possibility of some marital stress. Trust me, he wants you to be just as fit on your fifth anniversary as you were on your wedding day. Let an anniversary, not the wedding day, be your goal.

Vent frustrations or talk out phantom fears. Shed tears of joy and gladness. Have a designated listener. Not your mother. Not your father. Not your sister or big brother. No one in the bridal party. And certainly not your beloved. That designated listener may be a therapist or a cleric. Or you may have someone in your life who is a natural-born good listener, discerning, wise, nonjudgmental—and not "afflicted" with liquid lips.

You may be asking your attendants to buy dresses and shoes they may never wear again. One or more of them may incur travel costs. You are asking them to be all about *you* from the time you get engaged until you head off for your honeymoon. When it comes to gifts for your attendants, try not to make it yet another thing that is also all about *you*, such as a pair of earrings or a necklace you know is just the added touch to their wedding attire. Say thank you for *real*, with something truly thoughtful.

If you have seven attendants, you have seven different individuals with different personalities, interests, and idiosyncrasies. For that workaholic, consider a new PDA or handheld organizer. Is there a writer in the group? Track down a first edition by one of her favorite authors. For the fitness fanatic, what about a great active-wear ensemble and a Pilates tape?

If you cannot individualize, be creative and remember: never sacrifice quality for quantity. Pajamas, bath products, and scented candles are among the goodies sure to make most any woman's spirit rejoice (and feel appreciated). And no generic thank-you message, okay? Surely, you can take the time to personalize that.

If you have no bridal party, then there's only one major gift to shop for—that thank-you and I-love-you gift for your man. Surely you'll have no trouble counting the ways. An astute smoking jacket? Two tickets to the Kentucky Derby? A Cartier desk clock? That Armani suit you've been longing to see him sport? Some of my clients have gifted their grooms with luxury cars.

So many girls,
so many gifts.

chapter 11

budget-wise

Before you struggle to scrimp and save or max out your credit cards, think again. It's probably not wise or worth it. There is always a way to throw a fabulous wedding within your means. Have an intimate ceremony in the presence of immediate family and a few close friends—with you a vision of magnificence. After the nuptials, you and hubbie can celebrate by treating your party of, say, twenty to a feast. A wedding with a hundred or more guests is not the measure or ensurer of a successful marriage.

I specialize in the lavish but recommend you splurge only if you have the resources. A money crunch is a formidable marriage buster. To enter into your union with monster wedding debt is asking for trouble later on. So if you've said *Yes!* but cannot afford an extravaganza, marry now and have a full-out celebration on your second, fifth, or tenth anniversary. If you're not yet engaged but have dreamed of a big wedding since you were ten, start saving now, because your prince is coming.

Learn how much a big wedding will cost. Understand the cost of the details you desire. Be a savvy shopper. Consider your connections with relevant wholesalers or vendors. Consider, too, where you live. According to *Bride's 2000 State of the Union Report,* the average cost of a wedding in the New York metropolitan area was about $31,000, versus $17,000 in the Southeast. Whether you marry in Baton Rouge, Louisiana; Tulsa, Oklahoma; Austin, Texas; the Windy City; the Big Apple; or L.A., the issue is, What can *you* afford? Before you start shopping and laying down deposits, you absolutely, positively must count the costs.

Below, I offer an overview of the chief components of a wedding and the piece of the pie each is likely to take up, with the dollar amounts based on a budget of fifty thousand dollars. As you ponder the possibilities for your dream day in the context of costs, make a checklist—two checklists, perhaps: having both a WANT and DON'T WANT list may help you thoroughly think things through. Remember, it is *your* day to design as you wish.

Stationery, including calligrapher's fee: 5 percent [$2,500]

Go with a one-stop shop. Attend to all your stationery needs at one time to spare yourself the energy and expense of add-ons. If you have no interest in a full-out custom design, look for standard invitation packages to which you can add custom elements, such as a monogram or engraved motif. Engraving remains the Rolls of printing styles because it provides the best penetration of the color onto the paper and the crispest finish (result: optimum readability). If you don't want to go deluxe but want a step up from plain ole flat printing, you can have a raised effect with thermography. Another cost saver is to limit your printing to one color.

Your paper package will include all or some of the following:

Invitation Ensemble

Outer envelope: To slice and dice away a calligrapher's fee, if you have a friend with exquisite penmanship, call in a favor. Also, order 10 or 15 percent additional mailing envelopes to allow for addressing errors and changes in the guest list.

Inner envelope: Unless the invitations will be hand-delivered, as was the norm in the days of yore, skip the inner envelope! If yours is a custom order, you'll save a few dollars.

Tissue paper: Another holdover from the days of yore to guard against ink smears. Skip it!

Invitation: If your ceremony and reception will be at the same place, no need for a reception card. "Reception immediately follows" on the invitation will suffice.

Reception card: See above.

Response card: Instead of the usual:

M——————————————

—— will

—— will not attend.

(If you can manage it, have the calligrapher—or the friend with the fine hand—write in the person's name.)

One of the most challenging aspects of offering your guests a choice in entrée is that they will respond and put a check mark only next to the selection for all guests attending. So I try to make it as elementary as possible, using the following example.

————————————————
Invited guest

My guest's name is ——————————————

___ **accepts with pleasure**

___ **declines with regrets**

Choice of Entrée:

(Please provide each guest's initials next to the desired meal selection.)

___ **Mesquite-Grilled Filet Mignon**

___ **Pecan-Crusted Chilean Sea Bass**

___ **Pomegranate-Glazed Rack of Lamb**

(In the case of an invitation to Mr. and Mrs. X, they will know to leave the guest line blank.)

and fortysomething women do not get as giddy about being in a wedding as they did when they were eighteen. Do guys at any age ever get all that jazzed about being groomsmen? If these are your demographics, then you are really asking potential members of your bridal party to do you a very big favor. All the more reason for you to pay for their outfits. There's the gender-equity issue, too: guys can rent an elegant, fine-fitting tuxedo for a couple of hundred dollars, whereas women are likely to spend double that on their attire. To be fair to all, pay for all.

If you don't have a money tree, consider streamlining your bridal party to best man and maid/matron of honor, and perhaps a flower girl and ring bearer (children do add a special touch of joy and hope). Or you can take it a step further and nix the bridal party altogether. Just think, the money (and drama!) you do not spend on a bridal party can be applied to something you didn't think you would be able to afford.

Special family attire: If your parents and other guests of honor (godmother? granddad?) cannot afford new threads, be good to them.

Accessories: From the bride and groom to attendants and special family members, accessories may include a headdress, undergarments, shoes, handkerchiefs, and jewelry—including the wedding bands!

Hair and makeup: Depending on hair textures and styles, hair salon and barbershop appointments will be needed for you, your beloved, attendants, and special family members a day (or more) before the wedding. Ideally, you should also have a hairstylist, barber, and makeup artist on site the morning of. You do not want to run the risk of bottlenecks at barbershops and hair salons, especially if your wedding takes place on a Saturday.

Ceremony location rental: 3 percent [$1,500]

Church wedding? Many churches do not charge members of their congregations a rental fee, though there may be a fee for an extraspecial cleanup (or the expectation of a freewill offering). Before you get your heart set on a particular house of worship of which you are not a member, bear in mind that some of them will not marry nonmembers and some will not marry believers of a different faith.

Other ceremony options include private gardens, historical buildings, and an open bluff off a beach. Expect to pay a fee for sites like these, where prices are usually pegged to a venue's popularity.

Whatever your ceremony site, if you are thinking of bringing in outside talent—an organist or lighting technician—find out up front if the venue allows that or requires that you use their staff. Remember that, in most cases, just about anything is possible, but a venue is very likely to discourage the use of outside talent over in-house talent.

Some people think they will save a ton of money by having a private ceremony. But as ceremony space is not very costly relative to other elements, why deny yourself a great crowd of witnesses? If the ceremony takes place in a church, there is no need to rent chairs. If in a garden, most people will have no problem standing. The only reason to have a private ceremony is because you truly want only a special few to be a part of your sacred moment.

Reception location rental: 3 percent [$1,500]

You may save yourself money (and headaches) if you have the reception in a hotel, restaurant, or other venue that is fully equipped for entertaining. I think of the film *Father of the Bride*, when George Banks (Steve Martin in the remake) thought, *Oh, what a relief!* when his daughter announced that she wanted to have her reception in their home. He envisioned a low-budget affair, on the order of a kick-back-and-relax, gussied-up backyard barbecue. But his firstborn and only daughter wanted a much grander affair. Having the reception in the Banks home included the cost of putting a lot of their furniture in storage, freshening up the house and grounds, renting tents and tableware, and bringing in a caterer and waitstaff—and all their gear. In contrast, a reception at, say, a restaurant will likely be a one-stop shop (and in most cases, a wedding cake can be included as well). Rental of a room (or rooms) generally includes tables, chairs, and all china and glassware. Some places throw in linens.

If your sensibilities say no to a boogie-night reception, bear in mind that having an afternoon reception (generally noon to 4 P.M.) may well be a cost saver. Evening bookings (generally 6 P.M. to midnight) are usually at premium rates, as are Saturdays.

Food and Beverage: 30 percent [$15,000]

Yes, this is the largest piece of the pie. But here again, if there's no compelling reason to have an evening event, remember that lunch costs less than dinner. If you want your celebration to be an alcohol-free zone, there's another savings. And I say better no bar than a cash bar—that's a tad tacky. A gracious way to keep down liquor costs is to have a spirits-free specialty bar: say, wine and beer only; or champagne only.

Only after you have determined your budget and guest list can you start to think about whether you want to have a spread that works out to $250 per person or $95 per person.

Flowers: 10 percent [$5,000]

As mentioned in the "Flora" chapter, you can keep flower expenses down with arrangements that are architecturally driven. For example, instead of a full pavé of red roses for centerpieces, have a loose arrangement of red gerbera daisies. And there's my beloved hydrangea. One or two of these inexpensive beauties can do for a bouquet or centerpiece. Take into account a flower's fullness. With orchids, for example, you get more bang for the buck with dendrobiums than with cymbidiums. Choosing flowers that will be in season on your wedding day will also keep down floral costs.

Your floral needs may include some or all of the following:

Bridal bouquet: If you want to carry something other than flowers (a small Bible, for example), make note on your checklist.

Thousands of roses
await plucking for DeLeon's
lush ceremony altar.

Bridal toss bouquet: If you decide to skip this tradition, there's another small expense you eliminate. (And those little things do add up!)

Female attendants' bouquets: No bridal party, no expense. If you will have a bridal party but, like you, your attendants will carry something other than flowers, make that adjustment on your checklist.

Male attendants' boutonnières: Again, no bridal party, no expense. If you have a bridal party but follow my advice in the "Flora" chapter, there's another piece of change you will not be spending.

Corsages for special family members: Mothers and grandmothers simply love corsages. This is one tradition that—although I feel it is outdated—definitely should not be eliminated, or they will curse your wedding planner.

Ceremony beautification: In a church, for example, this may be for the center aisle and the altar area.

Reception beautification: Depending on the room, you may not need an abundance of flowers. In some cases, ceremony flowers can be reused for the reception. Those potted urns that line the church's center aisle, for example, can later frame the dance floor or cake table. (And when it comes to the centerpiece, you may find a less expensive yet still charming alternative to flowers, such as an artful display of candles.)

Decor: 12 percent [$6,000]

Aside from flowers, what other adornment will you want for a room? Total or partial recarpeting? Window treatments? Chair upholstery? What if you don't care for the chairs and tables that come standard with a venue? What about the dance floor? Will the standard parquet floor suffice, or do you want to jazz things up with a fire red dance floor?

One way to keep down redecorating costs is to choose a venue that meshes with your theme and so will not require an extreme makeover. For example, if you want to be in a contemporary zone, don't have your reception in a Victorian mansion. But if you are playing Queen Victoria for a day, that mansion's interior design and decoration—ornate wall sconces, green saffron taffeta or red velvet walls, triple wedding band mirror, Tiffany fireplace screen, Duncan Phyfe–type furniture—will reduce the amount of money and energy you'll need to spend on making the space a perfect fit.

Photographer: 5 percent [$2,500]

As I stressed in "Click!," don't skimp on your visuals. This is not to say that there aren't some ways to cut costs. If you have a friend who can handle simple shots, ask him or her to take pre-ceremony photos of you so you can limit the number of hours your photographer is booked. If that's not a possibility, ask about having an assistant photographer cover your preceremony moments.

Videographer: 4 percent [$2,000]

I repeat: don't skimp on your visuals! The cost savers mentioned above also apply to videography.

Entertainment: 5 percent [$2,500]

Your entertainment professionals may include all or some of the following:

Ceremony musician(s): If you cannot spring for a full orchestra, opt for a trio or quartet. Also, you may be surprised by the elegance of a single harpist. Whatever you do, do not play a CD.

Reception musician(s): If you can afford only one live-music experience, reserve it for your ceremony.

DJ: Take care to engage an ace DJ. When you contract with the DJ, ask him or her to give you a setup for the cocktail hour, which someone else can just pop in and hit PLAY.

Sound technician: Your insurance for a great-sounding day. There is nothing more frustrating for guests seated at the rear of the ceremony than to hear not a word of the vows. A sound tech will make sure that you and your groom, as well as your officiant, are properly miked. Having a good sound tech will also avoid embarrassing or clunky moments, such as the power going off during the reception because the circuits overloaded or people having to get up and walk over to a wired microphone for toasts because a cordless mike was not a forethought. And you certainly don't want the band or DJ to sound terrible. Most people don't know the ingredients of studio-quality sound, but they do understand feedback and speakers that crackle.

MC: Is Uncle Lenny the life of every party? Beware: he may be too loose a cannon for your wedding. To be on the safe side, hire a professional. Your DJ or bandleader can often double as MC.

Lighting: 3 percent [$1,500]

There may be no moments of your reception that call for special lighting (other than a little dimming, perhaps). Still, don't be so quick to skip lighting until you have considered how creative lighting can be a cost saver, as discussed in "Aura."

If you do want a little light magic, your venue's in-house lighting tech may not be suitable because he or she may be great at lighting for events such as business seminars but not so great at mood lighting a room.

Transportation: 2 percent [$1,000]

Transportation costs can include:

Rail or air: What if you, your fiancé, or members of your bridal party do not live in the destination city? In most cases, if you are paying for your attendants' attire, the out-of-towners among them will be happy to take care of their travel expenses.

Ground: If making your day will entail travel for many people, find friends who can do pickups and drop-offs. If that's not feasible, see if a cab company will let you buy rides in bulk: a 10 or 20 percent discount for, say, every ten trips from Airport Z to Hotel B.

Ground transportation also includes getting key people "to the church on time" (and to the reception). Here again, your decision on the bridal party will affect your transportation costs. If your bridal party is small or nonexistent, you may need only three cars for the high-key drives. Whatever your needs, remember that high-rent wheels add nothing. (Even everyday high school graduates enjoy limousine rides these days.) People you pass in that Bentley during your ride to the church may indeed stop and stare, but do you really get off on impressing strangers? When you pull up at the church, any guests milling around outside will pay only fleeting attention to the car. Their focus will be on *you*. In cases where there are many people to transport to and from the ceremony, I even go so far as to advise a mini or deluxe motorcoach buses over stretch limousines. If you must have limos, avoid the white ones. Isn't the prom over?

Favors: 1 percent [$500]

As I mentioned in "The *Wow!*," most favors are money wasted. They end up either in the garbage or in a Salvation Army–bound box.

Honeymoon: 3 percent [$1,500]

The south of France? Fiji? Australia? Morocco? Mali? A Caribbean or Alaska cruise? Or perhaps you prefer a brief, close-to-home getaway—a few days in a five-star hotel, a cabin in the mountains—with plans for a megavacation on your six-month anniversary. When counting the costs of your honeymoon, the items to list out include:

Travel package: For a cruise or an airfare-and-lodgings deal.

Customs or port fees: For international travel.

Rental car: Or maybe you won't be leaving the room.

Sightseeing: Ditto.

Tips: Always be gracious to those who serve you.

Wardrobe: First on the list—that wedding-night nightie!

Luggage: You may want to start your newlywed life with a new set.

Pocket money: In case you do leave the room once or twice.

Shopping: Ditto.

Et cetera, et cetera: 4 percent [$2,000]

There's always et cetera.

Wedding planner: If you're not a "detail" person, hire a professional. Look for a wedding planner who can offer fresh approaches to your celebration. But you want more than a dreamer. The wedding planner is the glue, the person who keeps all of the other components together and creates synergy among all vendors. In addition, a wedding planner should be able to offer you solutions to possible scenarios that might arise during the planning. For example, you may have your heart set on leasing a private estate but may not understand that this location could potentially double your costs, as opposed to choosing a hotel or resort with a built-in event space and rental items such as tables, chairs, and china.

When shopping for a wedding planner, look at past productions, get references from previous clients. If possible, find out what industry experts may say about a wedding planner. Most wedding planners charge a percentage of the overall budget. Some, a flat rate.

Event manager: If you are your wedding planner, consider hiring someone who will oversee the big day on the big day. The event manager's duties would include making sure everyone follows the script, supervising the handling of the gifts, putting out fires, and fixing snafus. An event manager could cost anywhere from one thousand to five thousand dollars.

"Office expenses": In the planning process there will be phone calls, photocopying, postage, carfare for vendor meetings and window-shopping, and other incidentals.

Security: Celebrities *always* need security because of paparazzi, fans, professional sleuths, and random snoops. Under certain circumstances, noncelebrities may need security, too.

Wedding insurance: If you are investing a substantial amount of money in your wedding day and if, on top of that, yours is the kind of mind that spins what-if after what-if—earthquake, twister, a venue going bust—purchasing wedding insurance may be in order.

Permits: Do not assume that you can do whatever you want without a permit. For example, if you want to marry in New York City's ever popular Conservatory Garden in Central Park, consider that making the reservation includes paying a permit fee for the wedding ceremony and an additional one for the photography session. It's not that the fees are prohibitive; the issue is that you should know the deal—the whole deal—before you start dream weaving. Not doing so can lead to disappointments. Does the park you're looking at have any prohibitions along the lines of Central Park's? Among them: no more than one hundred people; no "throwing of rice, birdseed, flowers, and confetti"; and no "alcohol, chairs, rugs, runners, and tents; amplified music and/or speakers."

For that custom tent you envision on country club grounds, know the 411 on occupancy and other safety rules. (Some localities prohibit lit candles in a tent unless the flame is at least an inch below the container.)

Lodgings: Will you have one, two, or ten people to put up for a day or two?

Gratuities: For vendors and others who go the extra mile, you may want to give them extra.

Officiant: Some have a set fee; others expect a freewill offering.

Premarital counseling: Some ministers will not marry a couple unless they commit to a set number of counseling sessions. Even if your officiant does not have such a requirement, you may want to do this anyway. How do you know how to make a marraige work if you've never been married? Consider the advice.

After you have made your checklists, let them get cold. Next, review them with your fiancé and other involved parties. If you have an eagle-eyed, very detail-oriented, disinterested friend, run your checklists by him or her for objective feedback.

And then . . . What's your budget? How much cash do you have on hand to earmark for your wedding? Twenty thousand? Fifty? Whatever it is, tack on 10 or 15 percent for unexpected expenses. That's your budget. Even if you're thinking *Money is no object!,* you should still establish a budget. No one has ever given me a blank check.

Establishing your budget as you dream your day entails taking a look at wild cards. Are you and your beloved paying for everything? Have your parents or his committed to contribute a sizable sum? Are there "angels" in your life? Would Godmother Bessie be happy to host your rehearsal dinner? Is there an uncle who long ago said that he would love to take care of a piece of your wedding expense? Perhaps he will pledge the flowers. If he says yes, don't go on a flower fling and then hand him a bill for nine thousand dollars. I know it's tricky talking about money with loved ones. But not talking about it can be disastrous. Know in advance how much that uncle is willing to contribute. Rather than take the cash up front, make a plan: when the bill comes due, he will pay the vendor directly. (Should the bill exceed your uncle's pledge, include your check for the overage when you send him the invoice.)

Other angels? Has your good friend the florist told you that whenever you get married he would be happy to donate his services (his time and creativity) and charge you only for his costs? Would Uncle Buddy be happy to give you a deep discount if you want to use his car service? Is there a professional photographer, videographer, or DJ among your nears-and-dears? Know who your friends "indeed" are and who among them has goods and services you can use.

But caveat emptor! Before you ask a favor or say yes to an offer, make sure your relationship is a control-freak-free zone. People are funny. Some give generously and freely;

with others, good deeds come with strings attached. One friend may go all out for you; another might have trouble doing her finest work—and following instructions—if there's no payday. Still others may have the best intentions but quickly become guests once the festivities get under way.

The wealthy can and certainly do have sky's-the-limit celebrations. Remember those November 2000 news flashes about Michael Douglas and Catherine Zeta-Jones's nuptials at New York City's Plaza hotel? Two million dollars, according to some sources (closer to three million, said others). You most certainly do not have to spend millions to have a magnificent affair if you make wise decisions at the outset about wedding party, guest list, venue, and a host of other matters—and if you make those decisions with a commitment to quality over quantity. The payoff for planning an affordable wedding—and sticking to your budget? Peace of mind!

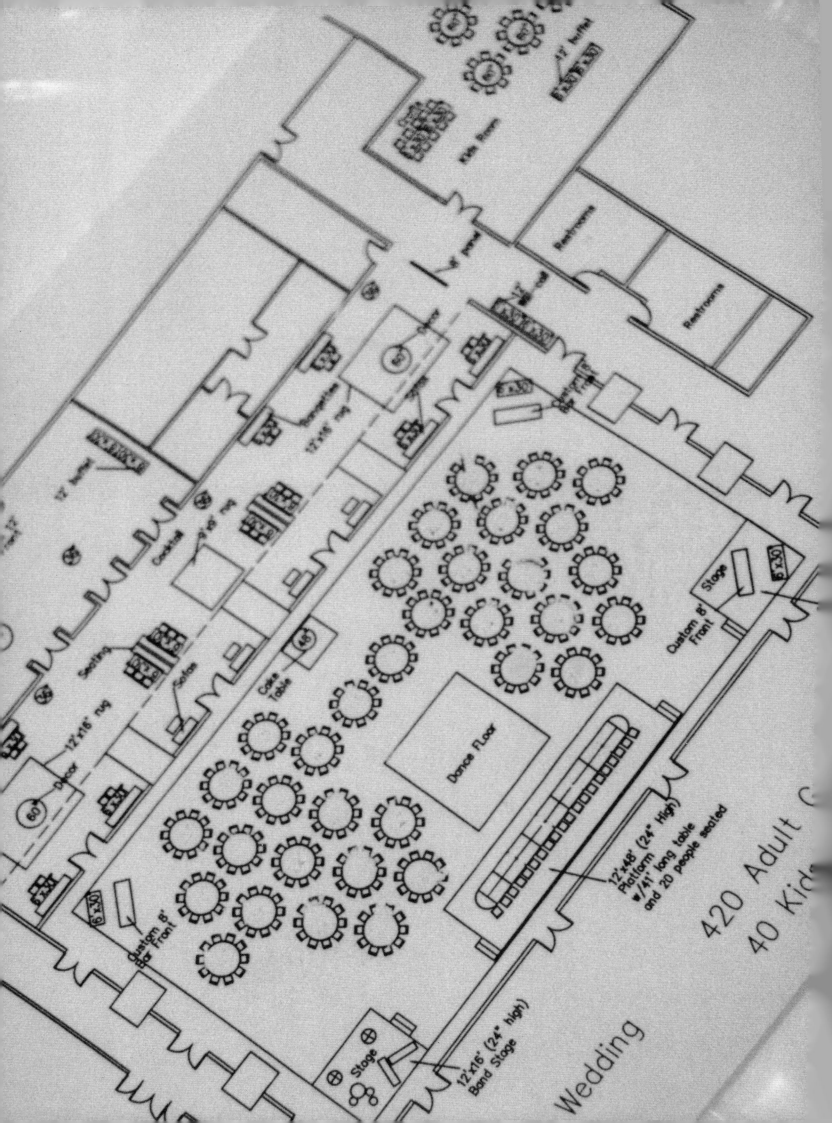

Wedding

420 Adult
40 Kids

12'x16' (24" high)
Band Stage

Custom 8'
Bar Front

12'x48" (24" High)
Platform
w/41' long table
and 20 people seated

Dance Floor

Custom 8'
Bar Front

Stage

Cake Table

Sofa

Seating

Décor
12'x16' rug

12'x16' rug

Cocktail

Kids Room

Restrooms

chapter 12

backstage,
valentine
style

Once you have established your budget and your check-list, it's time to make it real! If funds are in place, you can probably make your dream come true with six months' lead time, possibly less (and possibly more, depending on the complexity of your affair). Below, tips for the planning. If you are not your own wedding planner, may this advice empower you to keep your wedding planner on track and working in your best interests.

Envision

Meditate on the style and overall tone and energy you want for your day. High formality? Offbeat elegance? Casual chic?

Play Dress-up!

As you envision your day, dream on your attire—the inspiration for so much else.

People It

If you are going to have a bridal party, give your hoped-for attendants plenty of advance notice, laying out your expectations of them, so that they will have ample time and information to think it over before they commit. And don't assume that just because you ask they will—or should—say yes.

Next, the guest list. How large a guest list are you comfortable with? Two hundred? Fifty? Whatever your number, list all the couples and then all the singles, adding "+1" because no one wants to attend a wedding alone. (For heaven's sake, if you really want your single friends to come, allow them to bring a guest!) If you choose to include children in your celebration, make special plans for them. Have a separate child-friendly menu and special entertainment, possibly in another room. Make it so that the kids can be kids.

Location, Location, Location!

The Where often determines the When. The ballroom you have in mind may be booked on your first-choice wedding date—or perhaps it is available but the church you desire is not. It's important to secure your location(s) as soon as possible to increase the likelihood of having your celebration on your first- or second-choice day.

Yes, You Can but . . . May You?

Find out if any element of your wedding requires a permit. And don't forget that marriage license! Most states no longer require a blood test, and a license can usually be obtained in one to three days. Keep in mind that some marriage licenses will expire if not filed within thirty days. So be sure to read all the fine print.

Book Your Vendors

Contract with all the individuals and establishments you need to make everything on your checklist happen, from caterer, florist, and DJ to photographer and make-up artist. Do not dawdle. To secure top talent, you may need to book the person six months or more in advance. Remember, never, ever sacrifice quality for quantity. If necessary, scale back the scope of your wedding to get the best professionals your pocketbook will allow.

Organize It

Purchase a three-ring binder with indexable dividers, a pack (or two) of three-hole paper, and a pack (or two) of sheet protectors. Devote one section to each component of your wedding, from "Bridal Attire," "Ceremony," "Reception," and "Stationery" on and on to "Et Cetera, Et Cetera" and "Budget."

Use the lined paper in each section to log all communications, decisions, and transactions on items.

Use sheet protectors for the following:

- **Clippings and photographs of elements you'd like incorporated in your gown (the neckline of one couture gown; the bell sleeves of another, for example), your wedding cake, the reception space, and other aspects of the celebration.**
- **Correspondence, estimates, invoices, and other vendor-related paperwork. Having a paper trail on everything is a must!**

Budget Check

Every time you make a decision, reconcile your budget.

Make That Call to Attend!

The standard mail date for invitations is at least six weeks before the wedding. For save-the-date cards, at least six months.

Make Your Gift Wish List

If you are comfortable having a gift registry, plan on giving it a full day, as it is very time-consuming. Fortunately, many retailers now offer scanners so you can easily select items for your registry. However, you must still comb each department to personally select your preferences. Also, most retailers offer a limited online registry. But please do not insert gift registry instructions inside your wedding invitations. I believe that your guests should still have the freedom to buy you whatever they would like for your wedding. I always keep wedding registry information on hand for my clients, and most guests will call and ask. The only exception is when you are asking guests not to bring a gift. And for heaven's sake, don't even think about asking for monetary gifts . . . poor taste!

The Script

Your event prospectus may be anywhere from a few pages to thirty pages long. It should contain some or all of the following:

- **The names and addresses of your venues.**
- **Contact information for everyone involved, from vendors and technicians to attendants.**
- **Directions, including the best route to and from an airport and a hotel, and from the ceremony to reception.**

- A list of stage-managing matters.
- A production schedule: the step-by-step from Word Go until you depart for your honeymoon. Word Go may be the day out-of-towners arrive. It may be the day technicians and work crew commence the pre-set, in which case the event schedule would include information on everyone's travel and lodgings (as appropriate) and a timetable of all prep work, such as the delivery of carpet and the musicians' rehearsal. Word Go might be the rehearsal dinner or the morning of the wedding day. The final piece of the event schedule is a wedding-day time line. All vendors and your event manager (if you have one) should have a copy of the prospectus.

Your Dream Team

One of the most important elements is the team that you empower to execute your day. If you have friends who can help with some of the details, solicit their help. One friend may be the perfect person to take charge of the gifts. Another, mailing out your announcements while you are on your honeymoon (announcements that should be good-to-go on the day of your wedding). No element—no matter how small—should be left in the hands of anyone who is lackadaisical or a downright slacker. You want real talent. In some cases, that talent may not be a person's full-time occupation (say, a lawyer whose best hobby is calligraphy) or it may be bona fide professional.

In my years as a producer, I have worked with incredible talents all over the world, and I certainly have my favorites. They are the people who know what decision I would make in any given situation and who are not above pulling an all-nighter to get the production completed—the folks who have my back no matter what goes down. Make sure you have yours, because they will be your lifeline and insurance for a flawless production.

Beginning on page 256 are highlights from an event prospectus based on a wedding I produced at New York City's W Hotel. This prospectus features my top go-to talents, including Walter Hubert's production company, Silver Birches (SB), the muscle behind the magic, the hammer and nails that bring my dreams and imaginings to life. (Only the names of the bride and groom, and W Hotel's catering manager are fictitious. An actual D. R. Valentine & Associates event prospectus would include everyone's contact information—especially their cell phone numbers.)

People say never work with family, but I say always work with family. I could not have accomplished all that I have without the dedication and support of my sisters, Julie (left) and Mickie (right). Your little sister loves you!

Tina Thomas/Michael Holmes Wedding

Saturday, June 26, 2004

EVENT PROSPECTUS
FINAL DRAFT

Venue

The W Hotel

541 Lexington Avenue

New York, NY 10022

212.755.1200

212.421.3876

Contact: Carmen Carrero

(Catering Manager)

Production Designer

Peter Otero

Production Designer

Walter Hubert

Lighting Designer

Raymond Thompson

Musical Director

Earl Rose

DJ

Biz Markie

MC

Bengermin Davis

Producer

Diann Valentine

Photographer

Jasper Sky

Floor Manager

Kathy Marienski

Production Assistant

Donna Wisdom

Video Director

Paula Bond-Fitten

Transportation

Ricky Dunn

Production Supervisor

RaShawyn Morris

Makeup Artist

Eric Spearman

Travel Agent

Tracey DeFrancis

Stage Manager

Mickie Odom

Sound Technician

Joe White

Production Manager

Wayne Trask

Chief Financial Officer

Julie Dunn

Prep . . . Props . . . Preset

Crew Ground Transportation:	Shuttles will be provided for the crew from JFK to the W Hotel. Please see the transportation schedule for details.
Cocktail Setup:	See floor plan.
Dinner Setup:	See floor plan.
Climate Control:	74°
Check-in:	One 8-foot table on the break level of stairs that lead up to the 2nd floor of the hotel
No Smoking:	This will be a nonsmoking event. Please remove all ashtrays from event space.
Restrooms:	The hotel will assign one attendant to each restroom.
Amenities:	The hotel will stock the restrooms with the following:

- cloth hand towels sprayed with essence of gardenia
- minimum of 20 votive candles in gold-leaf glass votive holders
- milk chocolate mints in gold foil

Valet:	Valet will be hosted by the couple and provided by the W.
Hotel Greeter:	The W will post someone near the entrance of the hotel 3:00–4:30 P.M. to welcome guests of the Thomas-Holmes wedding.
Bars:	Two full nonalcoholic bars: one in the prefunction area to the ballroom and one in the upstairs lounge
Bartenders:	Two for each bar
Security:	Security will be posted near the stairs that lead to the 2nd floor and in the foyer that precedes the ballroom.
Coat Check:	The hotel will provide one coat-check attendant on the 2nd floor. All coats will be stored in the Waterfall Room.
Crew Parking:	The hotel has only valet parking.
L.A. Crew Parking:	All L.A.-based crew will be housed within walking distance of the hotel. Any ground transportation needs while in NYC will be provided by local taxicabs.
Rig Parking:	Parking in Manhattan is *extremely* challenging; therefore, unloading will happen curbside on the corner of 52nd and Lexington. Truck must unload between 1 A.M. and 6 A.M. Wayne Trask will supervise the unload.
Floral Storage:	FedEx is scheduled to deliver florals on Thursday. Florals will require refrigeration. Please contact Carmen Carrero to confirm a storage area.

Floral Workroom:	All floral prepping and work will be done in the ballroom on Friday. Please keep in mind that on Friday morning one half of the ballroom will be used for the wedding rehearsal.
Catering Menu:	See Banquet Event Order.
Bar Menu:	See Bar Prospectus.

Production Schedule

Friday, June 18

TIME	ACTIVITY	CONTACT
7–9 A.M.	NYC Truck arrives at SB for load-in.	Ricky Dunn/Wayne Trask
9 A.M.–2 P.M.	Truck load-in at SB	Ricky Dunn/Wayne Trask
3–4 P.M.	Truck arrives for custom dance floor load-in.	Ricky Dunn/Juan Gonzales

Saturday, June 19

Truck leaves L.A. for NYC.

Wednesday, June 23

TIME	ACTIVITY	CONTACT
	Truck arrives in NYC.	
10:30 A.M.	Floral shipment arrives at hotel via FedEx.	Wayne Trask
5:00 P.M.	DRV takes possession of ballroom.	Diann Valentine
5:00 P.M.	Truck arrival at W Hotel—New York	Ricky Dunn
5:00 P.M.	SB begins unload of the truck at the W.	Ricky Dunn/Wayne Trask
6:00 P.M.	Crew dinner on your own	
7:00 P.M.	DRV Production Briefing at W Hotel	Diann Valentine

Friday, June 25

TIME	ACTIVITY	CONTACT
7:00 A.M.	Sound installation begins in ballroom.	Joe White
7:00 A.M.	Crew breakfast on your own	

8:00 A.M.	SB crew begins installation in ballroom.	Walter Hubert
9:00 A.M.	DRV Production Meeting in Diann's suite	Diann Valentine
9:30 A.M.	Sound installation complete	Joe White
9:30 A.M.	Band setup for rehearsal	Earl Rose
10:00 A.M.	Wedding Rehearsal in ballroom	Diann Valentine
11:00 A.M.	Floral prepping begins.	Peter Otero
12:00 P.M.	Rehearsal Luncheon	Diann Valentine/Carmen Carrero
1:00 P.M.	Crew lunch on your own	
1:00 P.M.	Lighting installation begins.	Raymond Thompson
2:00 P.M.	Tree/Staging installation begins in ballroom.	SB/W staff
2:00 P.M.	W Hotel drops chairs in ballroom.	Carmen Carrero
3:00 P.M.	W Hotel drops tables on 2nd side of ballroom.	Carmen Carrero
7:00 P.M.	Ballroom installation complete for ceremony	SB/W staff
7:00 P.M.	Crew dinner on your own	
9:00 P.M.	Lighting Check	Raymond Thompson
9:00 P.M.	Alison Duke shoots ceremony room.	Alison Duke
9:00 P.M.	2nd half of ballroom set with storage of dinner tables.	SB/W staff

Saturday, June 26

TIME	ACTIVITY	CONTACT
8:00 A.M.	Crew breakfast on your own	
8:30 A.M.	DRV Final Briefing in Diann Valentine's suite	Diann Valentine
9:00 A.M.	Donna Wisdom reports to bride's suite.	Donna Wisdom
9:00 A.M.	Hairstylist arrives in bridal suite for hair setup.	Donna Wisdom
9:00 A.M.	Transportation pick-up of Eric Spearman	Donna Wisdom
10:00 A.M.	Breakfast delivered to bride's suite	Donna Wisdom/W staff
10:00 A.M.	Eric Spearman arrives in bride's suite.	Donna Wisdom
10:00 A.M.	Makeup Assistant arrives at bride's suite.	Donna Wisdom
11:00 A.M.	Breakfast delivered to groom's suite	Donna Wisdom/W staff
11:00 A.M.	Stephanie Jasper arrives at bride's suite.	Donna Wisdom

11:00 A.M.	Cocktail area is staged. Bars are set.	Walter Hubert
12:00 P.M.	Video crew arrives at bride's suite.	Paula Bond-Fitten
12:00 P.M.	Ceremony platform complete	SB
1:00 P.M.	Ceremony Complete!	SB
1:00 P.M.	Crew lunch on your own	
1:00 P.M.	Stephanie Jasper arrives at groom's suite.	Donna Wisdom
1:00 P.M.	Band sound check in ballroom	Joe White
2:00 P.M.	Biz Markie sound check in ballroom	Joe White
2:00 P.M.	Women's personals delivered to bride's suite	SB
2:00 P.M.	Men's personals delivered to groom's suite	SB
2:00 P.M.	Ushers/hostesses personals delivered to ballroom	SB
2:30 P.M.	Band Call Time	Earl Rose
3:00 P.M.	Hostesses/Ushers arrive for ceremony.	Mickie Odom
3:30 P.M.	Pre-ceremony music begins.	Earl Rose
3:00–3:30 P.M.	As guests arrive, ushers escort them to seats, leaving the first row on each side of the aisle vacant.	
3:00 P.M.	Diann Valentine and Donna Wisdom bring the bride and bridesmaids downstairs to the Sea and Ocean Room to hold for the ceremony.	
3:15 P.M.	Julie Dunn brings groom and groomsmen downstairs to the Arbor Boardroom to hold for the ceremony.	
3:30 P.M.	Pre-ceremony music begins.	
3:30 P.M.	Ceremony doors open.	
3:30 P.M.	Julie Dunn meets minister and brings him down to hold in the Arbor Boardroom. Confirm with minister that couple will recite personal wedding vows.	
3:55 P.M.	Guests are held in the foyer area until after the bride makes her descent down the center aisle and onto the platform for the ceremony.	
4:00 P.M.	Cocktail area is complete after the start of the ceremony.	
4:00 P.M.	Welcome	
4:05 P.M.	Seating of the VIPs to "Cupid"	
	Mother of the Groom	
	Godmother of the Bride	
	Mother of the Bride	

Groom's Processional to "Ordinary"

Entrance of Officiant

Entrance of Groom

Entrance of Best Man

Entrance of Groomsmen

Bride's Processional to "Jesus Is a Love Song"

Entrance of Bridesmaids

Entrance of Maid of Honor

Entrance of Ring Bearer

Entrance of Flower Girls

Entrance of the Bride

The Wedding Ceremony

Opening Ceremony

Marriage Vows

Exchanging of the Rings

Prayer

Presentation of Bride and Groom

Recessional to "Angel of Mine"

Immediately following the ceremony, the wedding party will return to the ceremony platform for
formal photos. Eric Spearman to assist as needed.

5:00–6:00 P.M.	Cocktails with music
5:00–5:45 P.M.	The Changeover

Once guests depart the ceremony room into the cocktail reception, the doors into the ceremony room
must be locked. The W will ensure that all doors leading into the ballroom are locked.

*Please be mindful that guests will be in cocktails and this changeover must happen quickly and quietly.

5:50 P.M.	Diann Valentine's final inspection of Grand Ballroom
6:00 P.M.	Reception doors open for dinner. W waiters should be on hand to help guests quickly locate their tables.
6:00–6:20 P.M.	Guests transition into dinner.

The wedding party can proceed into the reception with guests and to their seats.

6:30 P.M.	Introduction of Couple of Honor
6:35 P.M.	First Dance: "You Rock My World"
6:40 P.M.	Second Dance: "It's Alright, Send Me"
6:45 P.M.	First Course (Appetizer)

Salad dressing is served French style after all salads are plated.

7:05 P.M.	Second Course (Salad)
7:30 P.M.	Third Course (Entrée)
7:55 P.M.	Nonalcoholic Wine Service

After all of the dinner entrées are placed, the W staff is to serve sparkling cider. Each waiter should have a silver tray holding twelve champagne flutes and one bottle of sparkling cider for each table.

8:00 P.M.	Crew dinner in Canyon Room near the Grand Ballroom
8:05 P.M.	Special Toasts
8:40 P.M.	Clearing of entrées
8:50 P.M.	Fourth Course (Dessert)
9:00 P.M.	The Second Dance: "Hold Me" by Commission
9:00–9:30 P.M.	Open Dancing
10:00 P.M.	Throwing of the Bouquet
10:10 P.M.	Throwing of the Garter
10:20 P.M.	Cutting of the Cake
10:30–10:50 P.M.	Serving of the Cake
10:50–	Open Dancing!

Sunday, June 27

TIME	ACTIVITY	CONTACT
2:00 A.M.	Biz Markie wraps.	Monte Wanzer
2:00 A.M.	Sound strike begins.	Joe White
2:00 A.M.	Dancefloor/ballroom strike begins.	SB/W Staff
8:00 A.M.	Crew breakfast on your own	
10:00 A.M.	Ballroom strike complete for brunch setup	SB/W Staff
11:00 A.M.	Bon voyage brunch	DRV/W Staff

1:00 P.M.	Crew lunch on your own	
5:00 P.M.	Truck load-out complete	SB/Ricky Dunn
5:00 P.M.	Crew wraps!	
6:00 P.M.	Truck leaves for Atlanta production.	Ricky Dunn/Wayne Trask
7:00 P.M.	It's a wrap!—Thank you, Lord!	Diann Valentine

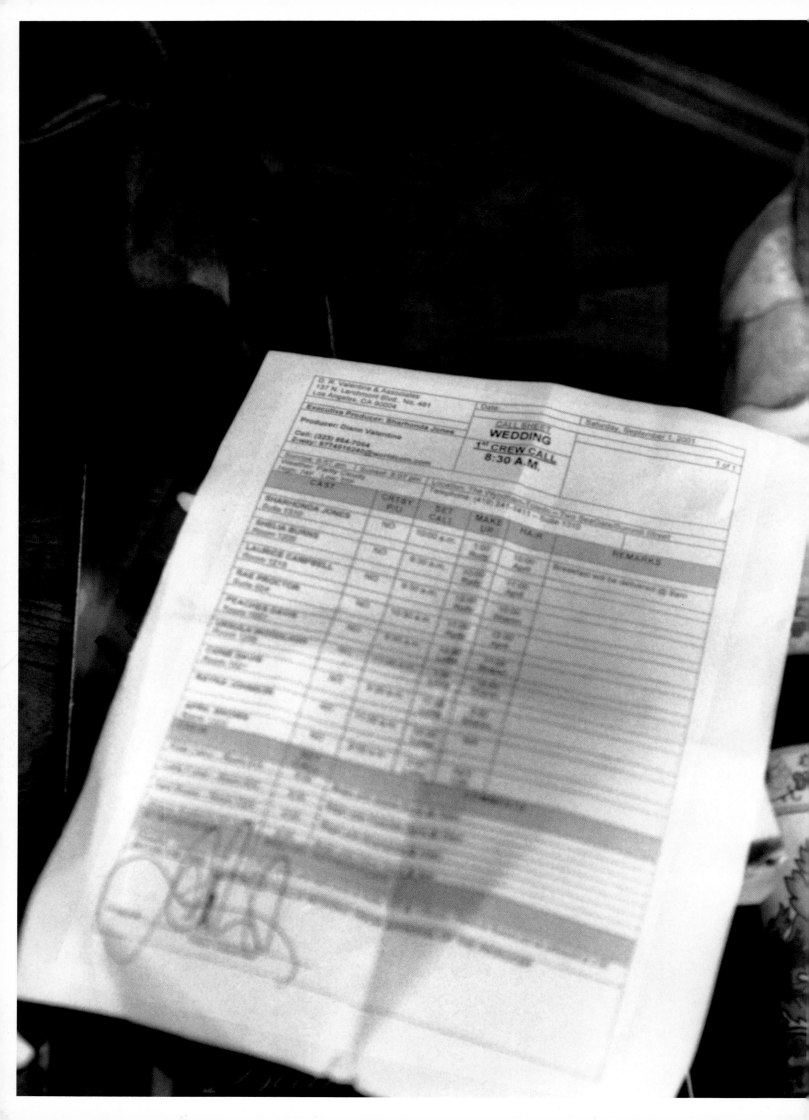

Opposite: Your bridesmaids should not be forced to wait around for hours for their turn in the makeup chair. Schedule their arrivals and services as precisely as possible. They'll love you for this. Remember, the day flies by only for you.

Above: DeLeon and I ponder her celebration, which is just hours away.

Above: Once the eighteen-wheeler arrives on location, our driver, Ricky Dunn, gets a chance to kick back and watch the production—and sometimes drama!—unfold.

Opposite: With Peter Otero, there's never a dull moment.

Opposite: Walter Hubert adds his
personal touch.

Pages 276 and 277: A rare moment when Gerry Garvin
allows me into his kitchen before a production.

Above: One of the most hectic times of the day is that brief period between the ceremony and the reception. Couples are excited, crews are scurrying, the photographer is trying to get everyone's attention, and I am sharply focused on keeping the production on schedule.

Opposite: Lighting designer Raymond Thompson starts setting the mood.

I say, every day is reason enough to be fabulous!

evolution

My career has taken me on an incredible journey in a relatively short time. God has shown me undeniable favor. I have been able to travel around the nation and the world in connection with my work, for the sake of creating beautiful memories for brides and grooms, memories they can revisit again and again during their days together.

I have experienced extreme highs and some pretty *low* lows! Through it all, what has kept me sane and focused is my faith in Christ. He has held me, encouraged me, provided for me, protected me, spoken for me, stood up and fought my battles, chastised me, patiently waited for my maturity, gently drawn me closer to Him, and gradually increased my faith. I have chosen to put my dreams in the hands of *the* dream maker, and He continues to do exceedingly, abundantly, above all that I could ever hope for or imagine.

Don't forget to pray!

When planning your wedding celebration, I urge you to keep God and your relationship with God first. Pray for your union; pray that God will keep it tight and enduring. Never forget that marriage takes work. Allow the precious Father to guide your lives down the path of marital bliss. Whenever I meet a couple still married—happily—after twelve, twenty,

fifty, sixty-five years, my first question is always, "How do you make it work?" More often than not, the answer references hard work—and prayer.

In *Weddings Valentine Style* I have allowed you to look through my eyes toward new and fresh ideas for planning the signature day of a sacred charge—a soul-deep, through-thick-and-thin, forever-and-a-day union. May you never lose sight of the love as you give full rein to your wedding-day inspirations.

So what's next for the girl who has always been in love with love? Along with ever-increasing faith, I look to bright tomorrows: to more offerings, of one-of-a-kind designs for I-Do days, and growing from designing a day to designing entire lifestyles—changing the game—for people who believe as I do: every day is reason enough to be fabulous.

Keep Spreading the Love . . .

Blessings

Lord Jesus—what a journey this has been! I now understand what faith is, because I have held on to this dream in spite of disappointments and devastating turns. And each time I thought it would never happen, you breathed life into it again and again. Thank you for giving me the desires of my heart. May this book be a testimony for those to see that when you put your dreams in the hands of the dream maker, miracles do happen. I love you with all that is within me. Without you, I am nothing.

To my super agent, Al Lowman, the take-no-mess genius in the literary world, thank you for believing in me and this project from the very beginning. To Tonya Bolden, my writer and who I now deem a good friend: you gave life to these pages. I am so thankful, because I believe God ordered your steps into my life. Thank you for accepting this divine assignment and for listening to my heart and bringing out the best in me. To Nelta Brunson Gallemore, guardian angel, for offering a keen eye and spot-on feedback. To my editor, Malaika Adero, for fighting the good fight for this project, giving it so much attention and care, and treating it as if it were your only responsibility. To Judith Curr, the most stylish woman in the literary world: when we met, I knew immediately that I wanted you to be the one to bring my book to bookshelves.

To Pop, my cornerstone, Richard Valentine, Jr., for always being my rock and the most incredible black man in this world. Thank you for all of your guidance and wisdom. I am so thankful that I have you. To Mom, with a heart of gold, Joann Gabriel, the sweetest woman I know: thank you for being such a shining example of godliness and for always showing me something to aspire to be. If I grow up to become half the woman you are, I know that God will be well pleased with me. To Angel Baby—Riann Morgan Valentine—for giving me a reason to get up every morning with a purpose. Thank you for being so patient while Mom travels the world helping women make their wedding dreams come true. You are growing into a wonderful young woman. I hope you are proud of this. I love you. To My Big Sister, Julie Valentine-Dunn, my best friend and my "always got my back" kinda girlfriend. Thank you for always believing that I could do anything, for never judging me, and for being one of the few people who really understands me. Pack your bags, girl—we're going places! To my sister Mickie, the prayer warrior, for always having an encouraging word from the Lord no matter how bleak the circumstances. Thank you for always being my right hand on the road—and this is only the beginning. To Quin for loving me but more importantly for loving and caring for my mother. To my little brother, Quin—I'm so proud of you. I know that God is going to do great things with your life. To Big Ricky because the road would not be the same without you. Thank you for trucking through rain, sleet, snow, and sometimes hurricanes to keep the production on schedule. To all of my family—Aunt Florene, and all of my aunts, uncles, and cousins, because family is the most important thing in life. A special shout-out to my nieces and nephews: Jasmin, Ricky, Bubba, BB, Kally, Jessica, Michael, Joe, Kayla, Lil' BB, and Morgan (Sugar Bunny). I pray that this inspires you to keep dreaming impossible dreams: you can do anything you say you can do.

To my girl Sherri McGee McCovey for helping me get this project off the ground when I didn't know the first thing about writing a book, but more importantly for always being a friend I could count on. I love you! To Carolyn Getridge because you may not realize how our brief encounter helped shape my future. I will always cherish our relationship and my first Gucci bag. To my small and tight circle of girlfriends, the ones who have supported me, prayed for me, and remained my friends through thick and thin—Lisa Clemons, Phyllis Bowie, Paula Bond-Fitten, LuTillian Hudson, Ladonna Hughley, Felicia Miller, Mandi Miranda, Lorna Kyles, Elise Neal, and Terri Vaughn—I love you all! To my mentor and dear friend Walter Hubert. You have taught me so much and unselfishly shared so much of your life with me. Your incredible sense of style and naturally fine taste take my breath away. I look forward to growing old together in that lavish Italian villa. To Mark Saltzman for willingly sharing such an important part of your life. To Peter Otero: mere words cannot begin to explain the depths of your creative talents. I am a better visionary and producer because of you. Thank you for being a part of my fondest memories in this crazy town called Hollywood. To Michael Daniels for your incredible interpretation of flowers. Most people don't get me as quickly as you have. To the DRV team (past and present) for your creativity, insight, and dedication: Amy Davis, Julie Valentine-Dunn, Ann Friday, Robert Hansen, Gary Hill, Pamela Gamble-Jackson, Mickie Odom, Clara Ross, and Donna Wisdom. To all of the professionals who have helped shape so many opulent weddings, because we all know that I am only as good as the team I have. To all of the hard-working people at Atria for putting up with my anal retentiveness to make sure this book is the best reflection of me. To all of the photographers who have captured the greatest moments in this book. Your interpretation is amazing, and I thank you for sharing your talents with me.

I have been most inspired by the women who have allowed me to share in the making of the most glorious wedding celebrations: Toni Braxton, Sierra Colbert, April Daniels, LaTonya Davis, Judy Dones, Lela Rochon Fuqua, Shawnee Jackson, Yolande Johnson, Kelis Jones, Chanté Moore, DeLeon Sheffield, Sharhonda Stockman, and many more. I celebrate you and all that you have given me. Thank you, thank you, thank you. And to D. Haley: thank you for giving me all of the wonderful things that my life has been missing. You've always believed in my gifts, especially when I no longer believed in myself . . . ride or die, baby!

Photograph Credits

Grateful acknowledgment is made to the following for permission to use illustrative material.

Pages 19, 25, 27, 29, 30, 34, 40, 49, 51, 60, 61, 73, 88–90, 93, 104, 107, 109, 110, 112, 113, 115–19, 121, 123, 124–27, 157, 163–65, 171, 172, 174, 177, 179, 196, 197, 202–5, 207–14, 216, 221, 222, 234, 244, 253, 254, 269–72, and 278–81: courtesy of Joe Buissink; page 14 (top and center): courtesy of Dan Chatman; pages 16 and 276–77: courtesy of Michael Dones; pages vi, 2, 6, 20–21, 26, 38, 43–48, 50, 52–58, 62–65, 67, 69, 71, 74–80, 83, 84, 87, 91, 92, 95, 96, 98–103, 108, 128, 131, 133, 134, 136, 137, 139, 141, 142–43, 145, 151, 153, 154, 158, 160, 166, 173, 175, 180, 183, 184, 188,190–91, 217, 218, 226, 230, 232–33, 284, 287, and 288: courtesy of Alison Duke; page ii (frontispiece): courtesy of J. Van Evers; pages 14 (bottom), 31, 33, 37, 120, 122, 138, 192, and 274: courtesy of Jasper Sky Photography; pages 146, 149, and 156: courtesy of Perfect Endings; pages 7 and 10: courtesy of Allum Ross; pages 155, 168–69, and 195: courtesy of Ross Standel Photography; pages 13, 22, 28, 32, 114, 152, 159, 186, 187, 198, 201, 225, 227, 229, 260, 273, and 282–83: courtesy of Simone and Martin.

Photographs on pages 9 and 15 are from the author's collection.